The Ultimate Devotional for Busy Men

David Powell

Beacon & Quill Publishing LLC

Copyright © 2025 by Beacon & Quill Publishing LLC

All rights reserved.

No portion of this book may be reproduced in any form without written permission from the publisher or author, except as permitted by U.S. copyright law.

All scripture quotations are taken from the Holy Bible, New International Version. Copyright © 1973, 1978, 1984, 2011 by Biblica, Inc. Used by permission. All rights reserved worldwide.

Contents

1. Adam: The First Man — 1
2. Noah: A Man of Faith and Obedience — 4
3. Abraham: A Life of Faith and Trust — 7
4. Isaac: A Man of Peace and Trust — 10
5. Jacob: A Man Transformed by God — 13
6. Joseph: A Life of Integrity and Purpose — 16
7. Moses: A Life of Leadership and Dependence on God — 19
8. Aaron: A Life of Leadership, Failure, and Redemption — 22
9. Jethro: A Life of Wisdom, Leadership, and Godly Counsel — 25
10. Bezalel: A Life of God-Given Skill, Purpose, and Obedient Service — 28
11. Balaam: A Journey of Compromise, Greed, and God's Sovereignty — 31
12. Joshua: A Life of Courage and Leadership — 34
13. Caleb: A Life of Unwavering Faith, Courage, and Inheriting God's Promises — 37
14. Othniel: A Life of Courage, Obedience, and Deliverance — 40
15. Gideon: From Fear to Faith — 43
16. Jephthah: A Journey of Rejection, Leadership, and Costly Commitments — 46
17. Samson: Strength, Weakness, and Redemption — 49
18. Boaz: A Life of Integrity, Kindness, and Redeeming Love — 52

19.	Eli: A Life of Leadership, Neglect, and God's Sovereignty	55
20.	Samuel: A Life of Listening and Leading	58
21.	Saul: The Dangers of Pride and Disobedience	61
22.	David: A Man After God's Own Heart	64
23.	Solomon: Wisdom, Success, and the Dangers of Compromise	67
24.	Elijah: Bold Faith, Spiritual Battles, and God's Sustaining Power	70
25.	King Ahab: Compromise, Idolatry, and Missed Opportunities	73
26.	King Jehoshaphat: A Life of Seeking God, Bold Faith, and Wise Leadership	76
27.	Elisha: A Life of Faith, Miracles, and Service	79
28.	Gehazi (Elisha's Servant): A Journey of Fear, Faith, and Spiritual Vision	82
29.	Naaman: A Journey of Pride, Humility, and God's Healing Power	85
30.	King Hezekiah: A Life of Faith, Prayer, and Renewal	88
31.	King Josiah: A Life of Spiritual Revival, Obedience, and Seeking God's Truth	91
32.	Job: Enduring Suffering with Faith and Trust	94
33.	Isaiah: A Life of Calling, Conviction, and Prophetic Vision	97
34.	Jeremiah: A Life of Faithfulness in the Face of Opposition	100
35.	Ezekiel: A Life of Vision, Obedience, and Restoration	103
36.	Daniel: A Life of Unshakable Faith, Prayer, and Godly Influence	106
37.	Shadrach, Meshach, and Abednego: Unwavering Faith, Courage, and God's Deliverance	109
38.	Nehemiah: A Life of Leadership, Prayer, and Perseverance	112
39.	Ezra: A Life of Devotion, Obedience, and Revival	115
	Make a Difference with Your Review	118
40.	Jonah: A Life of Obedience, Mercy, and God's Sovereignty	120
41.	Hosea: Unfailing Love, Faithfulness, and God's Redemption	123

42.	Malachi: A Life of Faithfulness, Honor, and True Worship	126
43.	John the Baptist: A Life of Purpose, Humility, and Boldness	129
44.	Jesus Christ: The Perfect Example of Love, Humility, and Obedience	132
45.	Peter: A Life of Boldness, Failure, and Redemption	135
46.	John (The Apostle): Love, Truth, and Deep Relationship with Jesus	138
47.	Andrew: A Life of Humility, Evangelism, and Quiet Faithfulness	141
48.	Thomas: A Life of Faith, Doubt, and Conviction	144
49.	Philip the Apostle: Seeking Truth, Growing Faith, and Witnessing Jesus' Glory	147
50.	Matthew (Levi): A Life of Grace, Transformation, and Calling	150
51.	Bartholomew (Nathanael): A Life of Sincerity, Faith, and Commitment to Christ	153
52.	James (Son of Zebedee): Zeal, Transformation, and Courageous Faith	156
53.	Judas Iscariot: Lost Potential, Betrayal, and the Consequences of Unrepentant Sin	159
54.	Simon the Zealot, Judas (Thaddeus), and James (Son of Alphaeus): Humble Service, Faithfulness, and Quiet Obedience	162
55.	Lazarus: A Life of Resurrection, Faith, and Trust in God's Timing	165
56.	Zacchaeus: Seeking Jesus, Repentance, and Radical Transformation	168
57.	Nicodemus: A Journey from Curiosity to Courageous Faith	171
58.	Jairus: A Journey of Desperation, Faith, and Trusting in Jesus' Timing	174
59.	The Centurion: A Life of Humility, Faith, and Trust in Jesus' Authority	177
60.	The Thief on the Cross: A Journey of Repentance, Faith, and Grace	180
61.	Simon of Cyrene: Unexpected Purpose, Humble Service, and Carrying the Cross	183
62.	Bartimaeus: Persistent Faith, Boldness, and Receiving Sight from Jesus	186

63.	The Rich Young Ruler: Desire, Decision, and the Cost of Discipleship	189
64.	James (the Brother of Jesus): A Life of Wisdom, Humility, and Faith in Action	192
65.	Pontius Pilate: Moral Weakness, Indecision, and Missed Truth	195
66.	Jude: Contending for the Faith, Warning Against Deception, and Trusting in God's Power	198
67.	Stephen: A Life of Boldness, Wisdom, and Faithfulness Unto Death	201
68.	Philip the Evangelist: Bold Proclamation, Obedience to the Spirit, and Transforming Lives	204
69.	The Ethiopian Eunuch: Seeking Truth, Divine Appointment, and Joyful Conversion	207
70.	Cornelius: A Life of Devotion, Obedience, and God's Inclusive Grace	210
71.	Paul: A Life of Transformation, Boldness, and Endurance	213
72.	Ananias (Who Prayed for Saul/Paul): Obedience, Courage, and Spiritual Restoration	216
73.	Barnabas: A Life of Encouragement, Generosity, and Faithfulness	219
74.	Mark (John Mark): Growth, Second Chances, and Faithfulness	222
75.	Luke: A Life of Precision, Compassion, and Dedication to the Gospel	225
76.	Silas: Encouragement, Endurance, and Partnership in the Gospel	228
77.	Timothy: Faithfulness, Discipleship, and Spiritual Strength	231
78.	Apollos: Passion, Learning, and Boldly Proclaiming Christ	234
The Big Picture		237

Chapter 1

Adam: The First Man

(Genesis 1-5)

Day 1: Created with Purpose

Scripture: *Genesis 1:26 – "Then God said, 'Let us make mankind in our image, in our likeness...'"*

Lesson: Adam was created in God's image, meaning he was designed with purpose, intelligence, and authority. He was entrusted with responsibility—naming the animals, tending the garden, and walking in perfect relationship with God.

Reflection: Do you recognize God's design and purpose in your life, or do you feel like an accident?

Challenge: Spend 10 minutes today in prayer, asking God to reveal more about your unique purpose. Reflect on areas where you can better reflect His image.

Day 2: Given Responsibility, But Needed Discipline

Scripture: *Genesis 2:15 – "The Lord God took the man and put him in the Garden of Eden to work it and take care of it."*

Lesson: Adam was given the responsibility to steward what God had provided. However, true responsibility requires discipline. His failure to lead and intervene when Eve was deceived shows a lack of spiritual discipline.

Reflection: Are there areas in your life where you avoid responsibility? Are there things you're called to steward but have neglected?

Challenge: Identify one responsibility today (in your work, health, family, or faith) that needs more attention. Ask for forgiveness (if needed) from God or other individuals, ask for God's help, and take a deliberate action to address that responsibility.

Day 3: The Power of Choice

Scripture: *Genesis 3:6* – *"...She also gave some to her husband, who was with her, and he ate it."*

Lesson: Adam had the power to say '**no**' to sin, but he remained passive. Instead of standing firm, he followed his wife into disobedience. This teaches us that indecision or passivity in the face of temptation is still a choice—often, the wrong one.

Reflection: Where in your life do you tend to be passive when you should be standing firm? Do you avoid hard conversations? Or ignore sin in your life?

Challenge: Take action against passivity today. If there's a difficult decision you've been avoiding, face it head-on with wisdom and courage. If there is an intentional conversation you need to have, set up a time and place to have it.

Day 4: The Blame Game

Scripture: *Genesis 3:12* – *"The man said, 'The woman you put here with me—she gave me some fruit from the tree, and I ate it.'"*

Lesson: After sinning, Adam didn't take responsibility. Instead, he blamed Eve—and indirectly, God. This lack of accountability damaged his relationship with both.

Reflection: Do you tend to shift blame when things go wrong? Do you justify your mistakes instead of owning them?

Challenge: Today, if you make a mistake, admit it immediately without excuses. Practice radical responsibility in all areas of your life. If you recently blamed someone for a mistake, ask for forgiveness and take responsibility for your actions.

Day 5: Redemption and a New Beginning

Scripture: *Genesis 3:21* – *"The Lord God made garments of skin for Adam and his wife and clothed them."*

Lesson: Even after Adam's failure, God provided for him. Though sin had consequences, God's grace was evident. This reminds us that even when we fail, God's mercy makes a way for restoration.

Reflection: Have you allowed your past failures to define you? Are you embracing God's grace and moving forward?

Challenge: Today, embrace God's grace. Let go of past failures and make one decision that moves you toward a new beginning.

Final Summary: What Adam Teaches Us

- **Day 1:** You are created with purpose—walk in it.
- **Day 2:** Responsibility requires discipline—develop it.
- **Day 3:** Passivity is dangerous—resist it.
- **Day 4:** Blame-shifting is destructive—be accountable.
- **Day 5:** Failure isn't final—God's grace restores.

Life Application: Take the next step to become the man God created you to be. Reflect on which of these five lessons challenged you the most and commit to applying it in your daily life.

Chapter 2

Noah: A Man of Faith and Obedience

(Genesis 5-9)

Day 1: Radical Obedience in the Face of Ridicule

Scripture: *Genesis 6:22 – "Noah did everything just as God commanded him."*

Lesson: Noah obeyed God's instructions to build an ark despite never having seen rain before. His obedience was immediate, total, and unwavering, even when others mocked him.

Reflection: Are there areas in your life where you hesitate to obey God because you don't fully understand His plan? Do you fear what others think more often than you obey God?

Challenge: Identify one area where you've delayed obedience. Take one step today toward full obedience, no matter how small.

Day 2: Consistency in a Corrupt World

Scripture: *Genesis 6:9 – "...Noah was a righteous man, blameless among the people of his time, and he walked faithfully with God."*

Lesson: Noah remained faithful to God in a world filled with wickedness. He didn't conform to culture but maintained integrity.

Reflection: Do you stand firm in your values, or do you sometimes compromise to fit in? How can you be more consistent in living out your faith?

Challenge: Make one decision today that reflects godly integrity, even if it sets you apart.

Day 3: Patience in the Waiting

Scripture: *Genesis 7:16 – "...Then the Lord shut him in."*

Lesson: Noah waited in the ark for weeks during the rain and flooding and for months after it ended. He trusted God's timing instead of rushing ahead.

Reflection: Are you struggling with impatience in any area of your life? Do you try to control outcomes instead of trusting God's timing?

Challenge: Pray and surrender one area where you're impatient. Choose to wait on God's timing with peace.

Day 4: Worship After the Storm

Scripture: *Genesis 8:20 – "Then Noah built an altar to the Lord..."*

Lesson: Noah's first response after the flood wasn't to settle down—it was to worship. He recognized God's faithfulness and gave thanks.

Reflection: Do you take time to worship and thank God after He brings you through challenges? Do you celebrate His goodness?

Challenge: Set aside 5-10 minutes today to express gratitude to God—either in prayer, journaling, or through worship.

Day 5: A Warning Against Carelessness

Scripture: *Genesis 9:21 – "When he drank some of its wine, he became drunk and lay uncovered inside his tent."*

Lesson: After his great faith and obedience, Noah let his guard down. His lack of self-control led to an embarrassing situation and family conflict.

Reflection: Do you tend to relax spiritually after a victory? Are there areas where you lack self-discipline?

Challenge: Examine one area where you've been spiritually or morally careless. Take a step today to strengthen your self-discipline.

Final Summary: What Noah Teaches Us

- **Day 1:** Obey God fully—even when it's hard.
- **Day 2:** Stay faithful in a corrupt world.
- **Day 3:** Trust God's timing—don't rush ahead.
- **Day 4:** Worship and thank God after victory.
- **Day 5:** Stay vigilant—don't let your guard down.

Life Application: Reflect on which of these lessons hit home for you the most. How will you apply it moving forward? Take a moment to pray and ask God to strengthen your faith, obedience, and endurance.

Chapter 3

Abraham: A Life of Faith and Trust

(Genesis 11-25)

Day 1: Stepping Out in Faith

Scripture: *Genesis 12:1 – "The Lord had said to Abram, 'Go from your country, your people and your father's household to the land I will show you.'"*

Lesson: Abraham left everything familiar to follow God's promise, even though he didn't know where he was going. His obedience was based on trust, not certainty.

Reflection: Are you willing to follow God's direction even when you don't have all the details? Where is God calling you to step out in faith right now?

Challenge: Identify one area where you need to trust God more. Take a small step of faith today, whether in your career, relationships, or spiritual life.

Day 2: Patience in the Waiting

Scripture: *Genesis 15:6 – "Abram believed the Lord, and He credited it to him as righteousness."*

Lesson: God promised Abraham descendants as numerous as the stars, but years passed with no child. Still, he believed God's promise despite the delay.

Reflection: Are you struggling with waiting on God's promises? Do you believe that His timing is perfect?

Challenge: Write down a promise from God's Word that you're waiting on. Meditate on it today, replacing doubt with trust.

Day 3: Avoiding Shortcuts to God's Plan

Scripture: *Genesis 16:2 – "so she said to Abram, 'Go, sleep with my slave; perhaps I can build a family through her.'"*

Lesson: When God's promise didn't happen as quickly as hoped, Abraham and Sarah took matters into their own hands, leading to complications and conflict.

Reflection: Are you tempted to take shortcuts instead of waiting for God's perfect plan? Are you forcing something to happen instead of trusting Him?

Challenge: Surrender an area where you've been trying to control the outcome. Pray for patience and faith in God's plan.

Day 4: God's Promises Require Commitment

Scripture: *Genesis 17:9 – "Then God said to Abraham, 'As for you, you must keep my covenant, you and your descendants after you for the generations to come.'"*

Lesson: God reaffirmed His promise to Abraham, but Abraham also had a part to play—faithfulness and obedience.

Reflection: Are you doing your part in your relationship with God? Are there areas where you need to be more committed to your faith?

Challenge: Make a commitment today—whether it's prayer, studying God's Word, or serving others—that strengthens your relationship with Him.

Day 5: Faith That Leads to Sacrifice

Scripture: *Genesis 22:2 – "Then God said, 'Take your son, your only son, whom you love—Isaac—and ...Sacrifice him there as a burnt offering...'"*

Lesson: Abraham was willing to sacrifice Isaac, showing ultimate trust in God. God provided a ram instead, proving He is always faithful.

Reflection: What is something you're holding onto that God may be asking you to surrender? Do you trust Him completely?

Challenge: Identify one thing that's difficult to surrender to God—whether it's a fear, habit, or goal—and give it to Him in prayer today.

Final Summary: What Abraham Teaches Us

- **Day 1:** Trust God's call, even when the path is unclear.
- **Day 2:** Be patient—God's timing is perfect.
- **Day 3:** Don't take shortcuts; trust His process.
- **Day 4:** Stay committed to God's promises.
- **Day 5:** Be willing to surrender everything in faith.

Life Application: Which lesson challenged you the most? Spend time reflecting on how you can apply it in your daily life. Ask God to strengthen your faith, patience, and obedience

Chapter 4

Isaac: A Man of Peace and Trust

(Genesis 21-28, 35)

Day 1: The Blessing of Being Willing to Surrender

Scripture: *Genesis 22:7-8* – *"Isaac spoke up and said to his father Abraham, 'Father?' 'Yes, my son?' Abraham replied. 'The fire and wood are here,' Isaac said, 'but where is the lamb for the burnt offering?' Abraham answered, 'God himself will provide...' And the two of them went on together."*

Lesson: Isaac was old enough to resist but willingly trusted his father and ultimately, God. His surrender foreshadows Christ's ultimate sacrifice.

Reflection: Do you trust God with your life, even when you don't understand His plan? Are you willing to surrender control?

Challenge: Identify one thing you've been holding onto out of fear. Take a step toward surrendering it fully to God today.

Day 2: Trusting God to Provide

Scripture: *Genesis 22:14* – *"So Abraham called that place The Lord Will Provide..."*

Lesson: Isaac saw firsthand how God provided a ram in his place. This moment reinforced the truth that God always makes a way.

Reflection: Do you trust that God will provide for your needs? Or do you struggle with worry and self-reliance?

Challenge: Write down one area where you need God's provision. Instead of worrying, pray about it every time doubt creeps in today.

Day 3: God's Timing in Relationships

Scripture: *Genesis 24:63-64 – "He went out to the field one evening to meditate, and as he looked up, he saw camels approaching. Rebekah also looked up and saw Isaac..."*

Lesson: Isaac didn't rush into marriage; he waited for God to bring the right person at the right time. His patience was rewarded with a wife chosen by God.

Reflection: Are you patient in relationships and major life decisions, or do you try to rush things? Do you trust God's perfect timing?

Challenge: If you're waiting on something (a relationship, career move, etc.), take time today to pray and surrender the timing to God instead of forcing it.

Day 4: Choosing Peace Over Conflict

Scripture: *Genesis 26:19-22 – "Isaac's servants dug in the valley and discovered a well... but the herders of Gerar quarreled with those of Isaac... Then they dug another well, but they quarreled over that one also...He moved on... and dug another well, and no one quarreled over it..."*

Lesson: Instead of fighting for his rights, Isaac chose peace, trusting God to bless him elsewhere. And God did.

Reflection: Do you insist on getting your way in conflicts, or are you willing to walk away in peace, trusting God?

Challenge: If a conflict arises today, take the higher road. Choose peace over proving yourself right and trust God with the outcome.

Day 5: The Legacy of Trusting in God's Promise

Scripture: *Genesis 26:24 – "...I am the God of your father Abraham. Do not be afraid, for I am with you..."*

Lesson: Isaac inherited God's promise not because of his effort but because of God's faithfulness.

Reflection: Are you striving to make things happen in your own strength, or are you resting in God's faithfulness?

Challenge: Take time today to remember God's past faithfulness in your life. Write down a few ways He has guided and provided for you.

Final Summary: What Isaac Teaches Us

- **Day 1:** Surrender fully—God's plan is always greater.
- **Day 2:** Trust in God's provision, not your own effort.
- **Day 3:** Wait on God's timing in relationships.
- **Day 4:** Choose peace over conflict.
- **Day 5:** Rest in God's faithfulness.

Life Application: Which of these lessons resonates with you most? How can you apply it moving forward? Spend time in prayer, asking God to help you trust Him more deeply in these areas.

Chapter 5

Jacob: A Man Transformed by God

(Genesis 25-37, 42-49)

Day 1: Wrestling for Control

Scripture: *Genesis 25:29-31 – "Once when Jacob was cooking some stew, Esau came in from the open country, famished. He said to Jacob, 'Quick, let me have some of that red stew! I'm famished!' ...Jacob replied, 'First sell me your birthright.'"*

Lesson: Jacob was known for his cunning and manipulation. Instead of trusting in God's provision, he schemed to take his brother's birthright.

Reflection: Do you try to manipulate situations instead of trusting God's timing? Are you striving in your own strength instead of resting in God's plan?

Challenge: Identify one area where you're trying to force an outcome. Surrender it to God today and trust His process.

Day 2: Deception Brings Consequences

Scripture: *Genesis 27:35 – "But he said 'Your brother came deceitfully and took your blessing.'"*

Lesson: Jacob's deception in stealing Esau's blessing led to years of hardship. Though he got what he wanted, it came with painful consequences.

Reflection: Have you ever tried to get ahead in life through dishonest means? Are you willing to make things right?

Challenge: If there's a past mistake where you've been dishonest, take one step toward making it right today.

Day 3: God's Presence in the Wilderness

Scripture: *Genesis 28:16 – "...'Surely the Lord is in this place, and I was not aware of it.'"*

Lesson: While fleeing from Esau, Jacob had a dream of a ladder to heaven. This moment marked the beginning of God's transformation in his life.

Reflection: Have you been running from something? Are you aware that God is with you, even in your wilderness seasons?

Challenge: Spend time alone with God today. Seek His presence and direction in an area where you feel lost or uncertain.

Day 4: Wrestling with God

Scripture: *Genesis 32:24-26 – "So Jacob was left alone, and a man wrestled with him till daybreak... Then the man said, 'Let me go, for it is daybreak.' But Jacob replied, 'I will not let you go unless you bless me.'"*

Lesson: Jacob wrestled with God, refusing to let go until he received a blessing. God changed his name to Israel, signifying his transformation.

Reflection: Are you struggling with God over something? What is He trying to teach you in your wrestling?

Challenge: Pray and ask God what He wants to change in you. Be willing to let go of control and allow Him to shape you.

Day 5: A New Identity and a New Walk

Scripture: *Genesis 32:31 – "The sun rose above him as he passed Peniel, and he was limping because of his hip."*

Lesson: When Jacob wrestled with the Angel of the Lord, God put his hip out of its socket. Forever after, Jacob walked with a limp, a reminder of his transformation. His struggle led to a new identity.

Reflection: Has God changed you through struggles in your life? Do you carry reminders of how He has shaped you?

Challenge: Take a moment today to thank God for the struggles that have refined you. Embrace your new identity in Christ.

Final Summary: What Jacob Teaches Us

- **Day 1:** Stop striving—trust God's plan instead of manipulating outcomes.
- **Day 2:** Deception leads to painful consequences—choose integrity.
- **Day 3:** God is present in your wilderness—seek Him there.
- **Day 4:** Wrestling with God brings transformation—don't avoid it.
- **Day 5:** Embrace your new identity—walk forward in faith.

Life Application: Which lesson speaks to your heart the most? How will you live differently because of it? Pray for the courage to embrace the transformation God is working in your life.

Chapter 6

Joseph: A Life of Integrity and Purpose

(Genesis 37-50)

Day 1: Faithfulness in Trials

Scripture: *Genesis 37:23-24 – "So when Joseph came to his brothers, they stripped him of his robe... and they took him and threw him into the cistern...".*

Lesson: Joseph was betrayed by his own brothers and sold into slavery, yet he remained faithful. He didn't let his circumstances define his trust in God.

Reflection: Have you ever been treated unfairly? How do you respond when life feels unfair? Do you trust that God has a purpose in the pain?

Challenge: If you're facing a difficult situation, choose to trust God today. Instead of complaining, pray and ask Him to use it for His glory.

Day 2: Integrity in Temptation

Scripture: *Genesis 39:9 – "...How then could I do such a wicked thing and sin against God?"*

Lesson: Joseph refused to compromise his integrity when Potiphar's wife tried to seduce him. He understood that sin is not just against people but against God.

Reflection: Are there areas in your life where you are tempted to compromise? How seriously do you take your integrity before God?

Challenge: Identify one area of temptation in your life. Make a plan to resist it by setting boundaries and seeking accountability.

Day 3: Holding onto Hope in the Waiting

Scripture: *Genesis 40:14 – "But when all goes well with you, remember me..."*

Lesson: Even after helping others in prison, Joseph was forgotten and had to wait years for his breakthrough. But he never lost hope in God's timing.

Reflection: Are you in a season of waiting? Do you trust that God is working behind the scenes even when you feel forgotten?

Challenge: Write down a promise from God that you are waiting for. Every time you feel discouraged, remind yourself of His faithfulness.

Day 4: Using Your Gifts for God's Glory

Scripture: *Genesis 41:16 – "I cannot do it," Joseph replied to Pharaoh, "but God will give Pharaoh the answer he desires."*

Lesson: Joseph used his God-given gift of interpreting dreams not for his own gain but to bring glory to God. His humility led to his promotion.

Reflection: What gifts and talents has God given you? Are you using them to serve others and glorify God?

Challenge: Look for an opportunity today to use your talents to bless someone else. Actively give God the credit for your abilities.

Day 5: Forgiveness and Purpose

Scripture: *Genesis 50:20 – "You intended to harm me, but God intended it for good to accomplish what is now being done, the saving of many lives."*

Lesson: Joseph forgave his brothers, recognizing that even their betrayal was used by God to fulfill His purpose.

Reflection: Is there someone you need to forgive? Do you trust that God can use even your hardships for a greater purpose?

Challenge: If there's someone you've been holding resentment against, pray for the strength to forgive them today. Let go of bitterness and trust God's bigger plan. Confess out loud to the Lord that you forgive them.

Final Summary: What Joseph Teaches Us

- **Day 1:** Stay faithful in trials—God has a purpose in the pain.
- **Day 2:** Walk in integrity—honor God above all.
- **Day 3:** Trust God's timing—waiting is not wasted time.
- **Day 4:** Use your gifts for His glory—humility leads to elevation.
- **Day 5:** Choose forgiveness—God can use even your suffering for good.

Life Application: Which of these lessons stood out to you the most? How will you apply it in your life? Pray and ask God to help you walk in integrity, faithfulness, and forgiveness, just like Joseph.

Chapter 7

Moses: A Life of Leadership and Dependence on God

(Exodus; Numbers; Deuteronomy)

Day 1: Overcoming Insecurity and Excuses

Scripture: *Exodus 4:10 – "Moses said to the Lord, 'Pardon your servant, Lord. I have never been eloquent... I am slow of speech and tongue.'"*

Lesson: When God called Moses to lead Israel, he felt inadequate. He focused on his weaknesses instead of trusting God's power.

Reflection: Do you ever feel unqualified for what God is calling you to do? Are you making excuses instead of trusting Him?

Challenge: Identify one area where you feel inadequate. Replace your excuses with trust—take one step forward in faith today.

Day 2: Trusting God in Difficult Circumstances

Scripture: *Exodus 14:13 – "...Do not be afraid. Stand firm and you will see the deliverance the Lord will bring you today..."*

Lesson: When Israel was trapped between the Red Sea and Pharaoh's army, Moses trusted God instead of panicking. God made a way where there was none.

Reflection: Are you facing an impossible situation? Do you believe that God can make a way?

Challenge: Surrender a difficult situation to God today. Instead of worrying or complaining, pray and trust that He will work things out.

Day 3: Learning to Rely on God Daily

Scripture: *Exodus 16:4* – *"...I will rain down bread from heaven for you. The people are to go out each day and gather enough for that day..."*

Lesson: God provided manna daily for the Israelites, teaching them to rely on Him every day instead of hoarding for the future.

Reflection: Are you trusting God for your daily needs, or are you trying to control everything on your own?

Challenge: Spend time today thanking God for His provision. Trust Him for today's needs instead of worrying about the future.

Day 4: Handling Criticism and Opposition

Scripture: *Exodus 17:4* – *"Then Moses cried out to the Lord, 'What am I to do with these people? They are almost ready to stone me.'"*

Lesson: Moses faced constant complaints and opposition, yet he responded by bringing his frustrations to God instead of retaliating.

Reflection: How do you handle criticism or difficult people? Do you bring your frustrations to God first, or do you react in frustration?

Challenge: The next time someone frustrates or criticizes you, pause and pray before responding. Ask God for wisdom in how to handle it.

Day 5: Staying Humble in Leadership

Scripture: *Numbers 12:3* – *"(Now Moses was a very humble man, more humble than anyone else on the face of the earth.)"*

Lesson: Despite leading an entire nation, Moses remained humble. He recognized that his success came from God, not himself.

Reflection: Are you leading with humility in your family, workplace, or community? Do you give God the credit for your success?

Challenge: Today, choose to lead with humility. Give credit to God and others instead of seeking recognition for yourself.

Final Summary: What Moses Teaches Us

- **Day 1:** Don't let insecurity stop you—trust God's calling.

- **Day 2:** God makes a way—trust Him in difficult situations.

- **Day 3:** Depend on God daily—He provides for each day.

- **Day 4:** Handle criticism wisely—bring it to God first.

- **Day 5:** Stay humble—give God the credit for your success.

Life Application: Which of these lessons resonates with you most? How will you apply it moving forward? Pray for strength to lead with humility, faith, and trust in God's plan.

Chapter 8

Aaron: A Life of Leadership, Failure, and Redemption

(Exodus 4,7,17,28-29,32,39; Leviticus 8; Numbers 12,16-17,20,33)

Day 1: Supporting Others in Leadership

Scripture: *Exodus 4:14-15 – "Then the Lord's anger burned against Moses and He said, 'What about your brother, Aaron the Levite? I know he can speak well… You shall speak to him and put words in his mouth; I will help both of you speak and will teach you what to do.'"*

Lesson: Aaron was chosen to assist Moses, showing that God often calls us to support others rather than always leading from the front.

Reflection: Are you willing to serve in the background without seeking personal recognition? Do you value teamwork in fulfilling God's plans?

Challenge: Look for a way to support someone else's leadership today—whether in your family, church, or workplace—without seeking recognition.

Day 2: Standing in Faith in Difficult Moments

Scripture: *Exodus 17:11-12 – "As long as Moses held up his hands, the Israelites were winning, but whenever he lowered his hands, the Amalekites were winning. When Moses' hands grew tired, they took a stone and put it under him, and he sat on it. Aaron and Hur held his hands up—one on one side, one on the other—so that his hands remained steady till sunset."*

Lesson: Aaron played a crucial role in Israel's victory by holding up Moses' hands. This shows the power of supporting others in spiritual battles.

Reflection: Are you praying for and encouraging those in leadership? Do you recognize the importance of standing in faith with others?

Challenge: Reach out to someone today who needs encouragement. Offer to pray for them or simply remind them they are not alone.

Day 3: The Danger of Compromising Under Pressure

Scripture: *Exodus 32:1-2 – "When the people saw that Moses was so long in coming down from the mountain, they gathered around Aaron and said, 'Come, make us gods who will go before us.'...Aaron answered them, 'Take off the gold earrings... and bring them to me.'"*

Lesson: When Moses was gone, Aaron gave in to pressure and led the people into idol worship, showing how easy it is to compromise when we fear rejection.

Reflection: Do you compromise your values under pressure? Are you standing firm in your faith, even when it's unpopular?

Challenge: Identify one area where you've been compromising. Pray for strength to stand firm and choose obedience over pleasing others.

Day 4: Taking Responsibility for Our Actions

Scripture: *Exodus 32:24 – "So I told them, 'Whoever has any gold jewelry, take it off.' Then they gave me the gold, and I threw it into the fire, and out came this calf!"*

Lesson: Aaron tried to justify his mistake instead of taking full responsibility. True leadership requires honesty, humility, and accountability.

Reflection: Do you take full responsibility for your mistakes, or do you make excuses? How can you grow in accountability?

Challenge: If you've recently made a mistake, own up to it today without excuses. Apologize if needed and seek to correct it.

Day 5: God's Grace and Redemption

Scripture: *Numbers 18:7 – "...I am giving you the service of the priesthood as a gift..."*

Lesson: Despite Aaron's failure with the golden calf, God still appointed him as the high priest, showing that failure is not final in God's eyes.

Reflection: Do you believe that God can still use you, even after past mistakes? Are you allowing His grace to restore you?

Challenge: Let go of past failures today. Instead of dwelling on your mistakes, thank God for His grace and step forward in faith.

Final Summary: What Aaron Teaches Us

- **Day 1:** Serve and support others in leadership—humility is key.

- **Day 2:** Stand in faith with others—your encouragement matters.

- **Day 3:** Beware of compromising under pressure—stand firm in truth.

- **Day 4:** Take responsibility—no excuses, just accountability.

- **Day 5:** God's grace is greater than your failures—walk in redemption.

Life Application: Which lesson challenged you the most? How will you apply it moving forward? Pray for strength to serve, stand firm, and walk in grace despite past mistakes.

Chapter 9

Jethro: A Life of Wisdom, Leadership, and Godly Counsel

(Exodus 2-4,18; Numbers 10)

Day 1: Welcoming and Supporting God's Work

Scripture: *Exodus 18:1,9 – "Now Jethro, the priest of Midian and father-in-law of Moses, heard of everything God had done for Moses and for His people Israel, and how the Lord had brought Israel out of Egypt... Jethro was delighted to hear about all the good things the LORD had done for Israel..."*

Lesson: Jethro was not an Israelite, yet he recognized and rejoiced in God's work. He welcomed Moses and his family, celebrating God's power.

Reflection: Are you recognizing and celebrating God's work in the lives of others, even when it doesn't directly involve you?

Challenge: Take time today to acknowledge and celebrate what God is doing in someone else's life. Encourage them in their spiritual journey.

Day 2: Giving God the Glory

Scripture: *Exodus 18:10-11 – "He said, 'Praise be to the Lord, who rescued you from the hand of the Egyptians and of Pharaoh... Now I know that the Lord is greater than all other gods...'"*

Lesson: Jethro responded to Moses' testimony with praise. His recognition of God's supremacy shows how witnessing God's power can lead others to faith.

Reflection: Are you sharing testimonies of what God has done in your life, leading others to praise Him?

Challenge: Share a testimony today with someone—whether big or small—of how God has been faithful to you.

Day 3: Observing Before Advising

Scripture: *Exodus 18:13-14 – "The next day Moses took his seat to serve as judge for the people, and they stood around him from morning till evening. When his father-in-law saw all that Moses was doing for the people, he said, 'What is this you are doing for the people? Why do you alone sit as judge, while all these people stand around you from morning till evening?'"*

Lesson: Jethro observed Moses' leadership before offering advice. He didn't criticize hastily but took time to understand the situation.

Reflection: Do you take time to understand situations fully before offering advice or criticism?

Challenge: Today, practice listening more before giving advice or making judgments. Seek to understand before speaking.

Day 4: Wise Counsel for Leadership

Scripture: *Exodus 18:17-18 – "Moses' father-in-law replied, 'What you are doing is not good. You and these people who come to you will only wear yourselves out. The work is too heavy for you; you cannot handle it alone.'"*

Lesson: Jethro advised Moses to delegate responsibilities, preventing burnout. Good leaders share the load rather than doing everything alone.

Reflection: Are you trying to handle too much by yourself, or are you willing to trust others with responsibility?

Challenge: If you're feeling overwhelmed, identify one task you can delegate or share with someone else today.

Day 5: Teaching Others to Lead

Scripture: *Exodus 18:21-22* – *"But select capable men from all the people—men who fear God, trustworthy men who hate dishonest gain—and appoint them as officials over thousands, hundreds, fifties, and tens. Have them serve as judges for the people at all times..."*

Lesson: Jethro didn't just tell Moses to delegate—he gave specific qualifications for godly leadership. Leadership isn't just about ability but about character and integrity.

Reflection: Is your character being developed to qualify for leadership? Are you looking for and developing godly leaders in your life and community?

Challenge: Choose an area where you can improve your character for leadership and take steps to change. Encourage or mentor someone today who shows potential as a godly leader. Help them grow in wisdom and character.

Final Summary: What Jethro Teaches Us

- **Day 1:** Celebrate God's work—rejoice in His power and faithfulness.
- **Day 2:** Give God the glory—testimonies can lead others to faith.
- **Day 3:** Listen before advising—seek understanding before speaking.
- **Day 4:** Share responsibilities—wise leadership prevents burnout.
- **Day 5:** Invest in future leaders—develop godly leadership in others.

Life Application: Which lesson spoke to you the most? How will you live it moving forward? Pray for wisdom like Jethro's—to observe, listen, and give godly advice that helps others grow in leadership and faith.

Chapter 10

Bezalel: A Life of God-Given Skill, Purpose, and Obedient Service

(Exodus 31, 35-38)

Day 1: Filled with the Spirit for a Specific Calling

Scripture: *Exodus 31:1-3 – "Then the Lord said to Moses, 'See, I have chosen Bezalel son of Uri, the son of Hur, of the tribe of Judah, and I have filled him with the Spirit of God, with wisdom, with understanding, with knowledge and with all kinds of skills—'"*

Lesson: Bezalel was specifically chosen by God and equipped with the Spirit to complete his task. His calling was not to lead armies or preach, but to use his creative talents for God's glory.

Reflection: Are you recognizing and using the gifts God has given you for His purposes? Do you take your skills for granted or do you recognize them as gifts?

Challenge: Spend time today identifying your God-given skills and talents. Ask God how you can use them for His glory.

Day 2: Excellence in Work as an Act of Worship

Scripture: *Exodus 35:31-32 – "And He has filled him with the Spirit of God, with wisdom, with understanding, with knowledge and with all kinds of skills—to make artistic designs for work in gold, silver, and bronze,"*

Lesson: Bezalel's work wasn't just about construction—it was about glorifying God through creativity and excellence. His craftsmanship reflected the beauty and order of God's design.

Reflection: Are you working with excellence, treating your work as an act of worship to God?

Challenge: Commit to doing your work—whether big or small—with excellence today, as an offering to God.

Day 3: Working Alongside Others in Community

Scripture: *Exodus 31:6 – "Moreover, I have appointed Oholiab son of Ahisamak, of the tribe of Dan, to help him. Also I have given ability to all the skilled workers to make everything I have commanded you:"*

Lesson: Bezalel wasn't called to work alone. God provided Oholiab and other skilled workers to join him in the task, showing the importance of teamwork in fulfilling God's mission.

Reflection: Are you open to working with others, or do you try to do everything alone?

Challenge: Look for ways to collaborate with others today. Encourage and support those who share in God's work with you and in your secular work too.

Day 4: Obediently Following God's Instructions

Scripture: *Exodus 36:1 – "So Bezalel, Oholiab and every skilled person to whom the Lord has given skill and ability to know how to carry out all the work of constructing the sanctuary are to do the work just as the Lord has commanded."*

Lesson: Bezalel and his team didn't build according to their own ideas but followed God's exact instructions. True service to God requires obedience, not just talent.

Reflection: Are you using your gifts according to God's guidance, or are you pursuing your own plans?

Challenge: Pray today for guidance in how to use your skills in obedience to God's plan rather than your own desires.

Day 5: Creating for God's Glory, Not Personal Recognition

Scripture: *Exodus 39:42-43 – "The Israelites had done all the work just as the Lord had commanded Moses. Moses inspected the work and saw that they had done it just as the Lord had commanded. So Moses blessed them."*

Lesson: Bezalel completed the work faithfully, and it was recognized—not for his personal glory, but for God's. His work was blessed because it was done in obedience and excellence.

Reflection: Are you seeking recognition for your talents, or are you using them to bring glory to God?

Challenge: Dedicate your work to God today. Whatever you do, let it be for His glory rather than for personal praise.

Final Summary: What Bezalel Teaches Us

- **Day 1:** Recognize your calling—God equips you for a purpose.
- **Day 2:** Work with excellence—your work can be an act of worship.
- **Day 3:** Value teamwork—God's mission is best fulfilled in community.
- **Day 4:** Follow God's instructions—obedience matters as much as skill.
- **Day 5:** Create for God's glory—seek His honor, not personal recognition.

Life Application: Which lesson stood out to you the most? How will you continue to apply it moving forward? Pray for a heart like Bezalel's—one that serves God faithfully, works with excellence, and seeks to glorify Him in all things.

Chapter 11

Balaam: A Journey of Compromise, Greed, and God's Sovereignty

(Numbers 22-24,31; Deuteronomy 23; Joshua 13,24)

Day 1: Knowing God's Will but Wanting Something Else

Scripture: *Numbers 22:12 – "But God said to Balaam, 'Do not go with them. You must not put a curse on those people, because they are blessed.'"*

Lesson: Balaam heard God's clear command not to curse Israel, yet he still entertained the possibility because of the rewards being offered. His heart was divided between obedience and personal gain.

Reflection: Are you seeking God's will sincerely, or are you hoping He will allow you to pursue your own desires?

Challenge: Examine your heart today. Are there areas where you know God's will but are still hoping for a different answer? Submit fully to God.

Day 2: Ignoring Warnings and Pushing Forward in Disobedience

Scripture: *Numbers 22:21-22 – "Balaam got up in the morning, saddled his donkey, and went with the Moabite officials. But God was very angry when he went, and the angel of the LORD stood in the road to oppose him..."*

Lesson: Balaam insisted on going with the Moabite officials despite God's previous warning. God allowed him to go but placed obstacles in his path as a warning.

Reflection: Are you ignoring red flags and warnings from God in order to pursue your own plans?

Challenge: Pray today for the wisdom to recognize and heed God's warnings. If He is closing a door, don't try to force it open.

Day 3: When a Donkey Has More Spiritual Awareness Than You

Scripture: *Numbers 22:28 – "Then the Lord opened the donkey's mouth, and it said to Balaam, 'What have I done to you to make you beat me these three times?...'"*

Lesson: Balaam was spiritually blind to what was happening around him, while his donkey saw the angel of the Lord blocking the way. Sometimes, we can become so consumed by our desires that we miss God's attempts to get our attention.

Reflection: Are you so focused on your own plans that you are missing what God is trying to show you?

Challenge: Take time today to pause, pray, and ask God to open your eyes to anything you might be missing.

Day 4: Speaking What God Says but Not Living by It

Scripture: *Numbers 23:12 – "He answered, 'Must I not speak what the Lord puts in my mouth?'"*

Lesson: Balaam spoke only what God told him, but his heart was not fully aligned with God. He outwardly appeared to obey, but inwardly he was still motivated by greed and self-interest.

Reflection: Are you saying the right things but not truly living in obedience to God?

Challenge: Ask God to align your heart with your words. Don't just speak the truth—live it out in your actions and decisions.

Day 5: The Consequences of a Divided Heart

Scripture: *Numbers 31:16 – "They were the ones who followed Balaam's advice and enticed the Israelites to be unfaithful to the Lord in the Peor incident, so that a plague struck the Lord's people."*

Lesson: Even though Balaam initially obeyed God by not cursing Israel, he later found another way to cause harm—leading Israel into sin through temptation. His compromise led to his downfall.

Reflection: Are there areas in your life where compromise is leading you away from full obedience to God?

Challenge: Identify one area where you may be compromising your faith. Choose today to remove anything that is leading you away from God's truth.

Final Summary: What Balaam Teaches Us

- **Day 1:** Obey God's will—don't try to manipulate it to fit your desires.
- **Day 2:** Listen to God's warnings—don't push forward in disobedience.
- **Day 3:** Stay spiritually aware—don't be blinded by selfish ambition.
- **Day 4:** Align your heart with your words—speak and live God's truth.
- **Day 5:** Avoid compromise—it leads to destruction.

Life Application: Which lesson resonated with you the most? How will you carry it out in your life? Pray for a heart that fully obeys God, not just in words but in actions, and ask Him to remove any areas of compromise in your life.

Chapter 12

Joshua: A Life of Courage and Leadership

(Exodus 17,24,32; Numbers 13-14; Deuteronomy 31:1-8, 34:9; Joshua 1-24)

Day 1: Courage to Step Into Leadership

Scripture: *Joshua 1:9 – "Have I not commanded you? Be strong and courageous. Do not be afraid; do not be discouraged, for the Lord your God will be with you wherever you go."*

Lesson: Joshua was called to lead after Moses, a monumental responsibility. He could have been overwhelmed, but God commanded him to be courageous.

Reflection: Are you hesitant to step into a leadership role because of fear? Do you trust that God will equip you for the task?

Challenge: Take a step of faith in an area where you feel called to lead. It could be at work, in your family, or in ministry. Trust God to guide you.

Day 2: Obedience Over Logic

Scripture: *Joshua 6:3-4 – "March around the city once with all the armed men. Do this for six days... On the seventh day, march around the city seven times, with the priests blowing the trumpets."*

Lesson: God's battle plan for Jericho made no logical sense, but Joshua obeyed without questioning. His obedience led to victory.

Reflection: Do you struggle to obey God when His instructions don't make sense? Do you fully trust His ways?

Challenge: Identify one area where you need to obey God, even if it doesn't seem logical. Take action today in faith.

Day 3: Spend Time in God's Presence

Scripture: *Exodus 33:11 – "The LORD would speak to Moses face to face, as one speaks to a friend. Then Moses would return to the camp, but his young aid Joshua son of Nun did not leave the tent"*

Lesson: Joshua enjoyed God's presence so much he would not leave the tent where God met with Moses. This is likely the reason for his leadership and legacy that followed.

Reflection: Have you learned to appreciate God's presence? Have you ever experienced God's presence?

Challenge: Ask God to help you experience His tangible presence in your life today and to birth a desire in you to remain in His presence as much as possible.

Day 4: Finishing What You Start

Scripture: *Joshua 23:6 – "Be very strong; be careful to obey all that is written in the Book of the Law of Moses, without turning aside to the right or to the left."*

Lesson: Joshua led with perseverance. He didn't just start strong—he finished well by keeping God's commands.

Reflection: Are there areas in your life where you've started strong but struggled to follow through? How can you stay committed?

Challenge: Choose one unfinished goal (spiritual, personal, or professional) and commit to making progress on it today.

Day 5: Leave a Legacy of Faith

Scripture: *Joshua 24:15 – "…But as for me and my household, we will serve the Lord."*

Lesson: Joshua's final words were a declaration of faith. He set a standard for his family and nation to follow.

Reflection: What kind of legacy are you building? How will your faith impact future generations?

Challenge: Make a conscious decision to influence others positively through your faith. Take one action today to set a godly example in your home or community.

Final Summary: What Joshua Teaches Us

- **Day 1:** Step into leadership with courage—God is with you.
- **Day 2:** Obey God completely—even when it doesn't make sense.
- **Day 3:** Spend time in God's presence.
- **Day 4:** Finish what you start—persevere in faith.
- **Day 5:** Build a lasting legacy of faith.

Life Application: Which lesson spoke to you the most? How will you incorporate it into your life moving forward? Pray for strength to walk in faith, obedience, and perseverance like Joshua.

Chapter 13

Caleb: A Life of Unwavering Faith, Courage, and Inheriting God's Promises

(Numbers 13-14; Deuteronomy 1:34-36; Joshua 14-15)

Day 1: A Different Spirit of Faith

Scripture: *Numbers 14:24 – "But because My servant Caleb has a different spirit and follows Me wholeheartedly, I will bring him into the land he went to, and his descendants will inherit it."*

Lesson: Caleb stood out because of his "different spirit"—a spirit of unwavering faith and wholehearted devotion to God. While others doubted, Caleb trusted God's promise.

Reflection: Are you following God wholeheartedly, or is your faith influenced by fear or doubt?

Challenge: Commit to trusting God today, regardless of circumstances. Speak words of faith and refuse to entertain doubt or negativity.

Day 2: Courage to Stand Against the Crowd

Scripture: *Numbers 13:30 – "Then Caleb silenced the people before Moses and said, 'We should go up and take possession of the land, for we can certainly do it.'"*

Lesson: Caleb boldly stood against the fear-filled report of the other spies. He was willing to be in the minority, standing for God's promise even when it was unpopular.

Reflection: Are you willing to stand for God's truth and promises, even if it means standing alone?

Challenge: Be bold in your faith today. Speak truth and encouragement, even if it goes against the crowd.

Day 3: Seeing Through the Eyes of Faith

Scripture: *Numbers 14:7-8 – "...The land we passed through and explored is exceedingly good. If the Lord is pleased with us, He will lead us into that land, a land flowing with milk and honey, and will give it to us."*

Lesson: Caleb saw the same giants and challenges as the other spies, but his perspective was different. He focused on God's power and promise, not the obstacles.

Reflection: Are you focusing on the giants in your life, or are you trusting God's promises and power?

Challenge: Change your perspective today. Speak God's promises over your challenges and see them through the eyes of faith.

Day 4: Persevering with Patience and Faithfulness

Scripture: *Joshua 14:10-11 – "Now then, just as the Lord promised, He has kept me alive for forty-five years... So here I am today, eighty-five years old! I am still as strong today as the day Moses sent me out..."*

Lesson: Caleb waited 45 years for God's promise to be fulfilled. He remained faithful and patient, never losing hope or enthusiasm.

Reflection: Are you waiting on God's promise with patience and faithfulness, or are you growing weary and discouraged?

Challenge: If you're in a season of waiting, choose to wait with hope and faith. Remind yourself of God's faithfulness in the past.

Day 5: Claiming God's Promises with Boldness

Scripture: *Joshua 14:12 – "Now give me this hill country that the Lord promised me that day. You yourself heard then that the Anakites were there and their cities were large and fortified, but, the Lord helping me, I will drive them out just as He said."*

Lesson: Caleb boldly claimed the promise God had given him, even though giants still occupied the land. He trusted God to help him conquer every obstacle.

Reflection: Are you boldly claiming God's promises, or are you hesitant because of the challenges you see?

Challenge: Claim a promise from God today. Speak it boldly and trust God to help you overcome any obstacles.

Final Summary: What Caleb Teaches Us

- **Day 1:** Follow God wholeheartedly—be unwavering in faith.

- **Day 2:** Stand for God's truth—be bold, even when you're in the minority.

- **Day 3:** See through the eyes of faith—focus on God's power, not the giants.

- **Day 4:** Wait patiently and faithfully—trust God's timing.

- **Day 5:** Claim God's promises boldly—trust Him to conquer the obstacles.

Life Application: Which lesson challenged you the most? How will you continue to live it out? Pray for a heart like Caleb's—full of faith, courage, and perseverance, ready to claim God's promises no matter the challenges.

Chapter 14

Othniel: A Life of Courage, Obedience, and Deliverance

(Judges 3)

Day 1: Stepping Up When Others Won't

Scripture: *Judges 3:9* – *"But when they cried out to the Lord, He raised up for them a deliverer, Othniel son of Kenaz, Caleb's younger brother, who saved them."*

Lesson: Othniel was the first judge of Israel, stepping up when the people cried out to God for help. He didn't wait for someone else to act—he obeyed God's call to lead and deliver Israel. **Note**: Jephunneh, Caleb's and Kenaz's father, was a Kenizzite. The Kenizzites are one of the people groups God told Abraham his descendants would displace when they came into the Promised Land. (Joshua 14:6 and Genesis 15:19). This means the first judge over Israel was not even a "pure" Israelite.

Reflection: Are you willing to step up when God calls, or are you waiting for someone else to take action? Do you find excuses as to why you are not the right one?

Challenge: Look for an opportunity to take the lead today—whether in your family, church, or workplace. Be bold and step into the role God has for you.

Day 2: Empowered by the Spirit of God

Scripture: *Judges 3:10* – *"The Spirit of the Lord came on him, so that he became Israel's judge and went to war. The Lord gave Cushan-Rishathaim king of Aram into the hands of Othniel, who overpowered him."*

Lesson: Othniel didn't rely on his own strength; he was empowered by the Spirit of God. His victory came because he allowed God to work through him.

Reflection: Are you trying to do things in your own strength, or are you relying on the Holy Spirit?

Challenge: Ask the Holy Spirit to guide and strengthen you today. Rely on God's power instead of your own efforts.

Day 3: Faithfulness Leads to Victory

Scripture: *Judges 3:10-11 – "...The Lord gave Cushan-Rishathaim king of Aram into the hands of Othniel, who overpowered him. So the land had peace for forty years, until Othniel son of Kenaz died."*

Lesson: Because of Othniel's obedience, Israel experienced peace for 40 years. His faithfulness to God resulted in victory, stability, and blessing for the nation.

Reflection: Is your faithfulness leading others toward peace, or are your actions bringing confusion and instability?

Challenge: Be intentional today about making choices that bring peace and stability to those around you.

Day 4: Strength Through Spiritual Heritage

Scripture: *Judges 1:12-13 – "And Caleb said, 'I will give my daughter Aksah in marriage to the man who attacks and captures Kiriath Sepher.' Othniel son of Kenaz, Caleb's younger brother, took it; so Caleb gave his daughter Aksah to him in marriage."*

Lesson: Othniel was influenced by Caleb, a man known for his faith and courage. He followed the example of bold faithfulness that was passed down to him.

Reflection: Are you learning from godly influences in your life, and are you setting a godly example for others?

Challenge: Find a mentor or role model today who can help you grow in faith, and be that person for someone else.

Day 5: The Power of Crying Out to God

Scripture: *Judges 3:9 – "But when they cried out to the Lord, He raised up for them a deliverer, Othniel son of Kenaz, Caleb's younger brother, who saved them."*

Lesson: God responded to Israel's cry for help by raising up Othniel. This shows that when we sincerely cry out to God, He answers and provides a way forward.

Reflection: Are you bringing your struggles to God, or are you trying to fix them on your own?

Challenge: Spend intentional time in prayer today, crying out to God for His help and guidance in any situation you are facing.

Final Summary: What Othniel Teaches Us

- **Day 1:** Step up in faith—don't wait for someone else to lead.
- **Day 2:** Rely on the Holy Spirit—victory comes through God's power.
- **Day 3:** Stay faithful—your obedience impacts others.
- **Day 4:** Learn from godly examples—spiritual heritage matters.
- **Day 5:** Cry out to God—He hears and delivers.

Life Application: Which lesson stood out to you the most? How will it affect your choices moving forward? Pray for a heart like Othniel's—one that steps up in faith, relies on God's power, and leads others to victory and peace.

Chapter 15

Gideon: From Fear to Faith

(Judges 6-8)

Day 1: God Sees More in You Than You See in Yourself

Scripture: *Judges 6:12 – "When the angel of the Lord appeared to Gideon, he said, 'The Lord is with you, mighty warrior.'"*

Lesson: Gideon saw himself as weak and insignificant, but God saw a mighty warrior. His identity wasn't based on his past or weaknesses but on God's calling.

Reflection: Do you ever feel unqualified for what God is calling you to do? Are you limiting yourself because of fear or insecurity?

Challenge: Write down one area where you feel inadequate. Ask God to show you how He sees you, listen to what He says, and take one step of faith in that area today.

Day 2: Obedience Before the Battle

Scripture: *Judges 6:25 – "…Tear down your father's altar to Baal and cut down the Asherah pole beside it…"*

Lesson: Before Gideon could lead Israel in victory, he had to remove the idols in his own home. Spiritual battles require preparation and obedience.

Reflection: Are there "idols" (things that take priority over God) in your life that need to be torn down before you can walk in victory?

Challenge: Identify one habit, distraction, or mindset that has become an idol in your life. Make a decision to remove or change it today.

Day 3: Trusting God Even When It Doesn't Make Sense

Scripture: *Judges 7:7 – "The Lord said to Gideon, 'With the three hundred men that lapped, I will save you and give the Midianites into your hands...'"*

Lesson: God reduced Gideon's army from 32,000 to 300, showing that victory depends on His power, not human strength.

Reflection: Do you trust God even when His ways don't make sense? Are you relying on your own resources instead of His provision?

Challenge: Surrender an area of your life where you've been relying on your own strength instead of trusting God. Choose faith over fear today.

Day 4: Giving Credit to God for Your Victories

Scripture: *Judges 7:20 – "...they shouted, 'A sword for the LORD and for Gideon!'"*

Lesson: Gideon's victory wasn't about his strength but about God's power. True success comes from giving God the credit, not taking it for ourselves.

Reflection: Do you take credit for your achievements, or do you acknowledge God as the source of your success?

Challenge: Today, take time to thank God for your past victories. Give Him the credit for what He has done in your life.

Day 5: Finishing Strong—Avoiding the Pitfalls of Success

Scripture: *Judges 8:27 – "Gideon made the gold into an ephod, which he placed in Ophrah, his town. All Israel prostituted themselves by worshiping it there, and it became a snare to Gideon and his family."*

Lesson: Gideon started strong but ended poorly. After his victory, he made an idol that led Israel into sin. Success can be dangerous if it leads us away from God.

Reflection: Are you staying close to God, even after your victories? Are you guarding your heart against pride and complacency?

Challenge: Examine your spiritual life. Are you still seeking God as passionately as you did in times of struggle? Renew your commitment to putting Him first.

Final Summary: What Gideon Teaches Us

- **Day 1:** God sees more in you than you see in yourself.
- **Day 2:** Obedience prepares you for victory.
- **Day 3:** Trust God, even when His ways don't make sense.
- **Day 4:** Give God credit for your victories.
- **Day 5:** Stay faithful after success—don't let pride lead you astray.

Life Application: Which of these lessons resonates with you the most? How will you apply it moving forward? Pray for the courage to trust God, obey Him fully, and stay humble in success.

Chapter 16

Jephthah: A Journey of Rejection, Leadership, and Costly Commitments

(Judges 11-12)

Day 1: Overcoming Rejection and Rising to Leadership

Scripture: *Judges 11:1-2 – "Jephthah the Gileadite was a mighty warrior. His father was Gilead; his mother was a prostitute. Gilead's wife also bore him sons, and when they were grown up, they drove Jephthah away. 'You are not going to get any inheritance in our family,' they said, 'because you are the son of another woman.'"*

Lesson: Jephthah was rejected by his own family because of his background. Despite this, God still had a plan for him. His past didn't define his future.

Reflection: Are you letting past rejections or circumstances limit what God wants to do in your life?

Challenge: If you've experienced rejection, give it to God today and forgive the people who rejected you out loud. Ask Him to help you move forward in faith, knowing He can use you for His purposes no matter your past.

Day 2: Called Back When Needed

Scripture: *Judges 11:5-6 – "The elders of Gilead went to get Jephthah from the land of Tob. 'Come,' they said, 'be our commander, so we can fight the Ammonites.'"*

Lesson: The same people who rejected Jephthah later sought his help in a time of crisis. His skills and leadership, once overlooked, became essential.

Reflection: Are you preparing yourself for the opportunities God will bring, even when others don't recognize your potential now?

Challenge: Focus on growing in wisdom, skill, and character today, even if you feel overlooked. Your time for leadership will come.

Day 3: Making Vows to God

Scripture: *Judges 11:30-31 – "And Jephthah made a vow to the Lord: 'If You give the Ammonites into my hands, whatever comes out of the door of my house to meet me when I return in triumph from the Ammonites will be the Lord's, and I will sacrifice it as a burnt offering.'"*

Lesson: Jephthah made a rash vow, seeking to bargain with God rather than trusting Him completely. His words had unintended consequences.

Reflection: Are you careful with the promises and commitments you make to God and others?

Challenge: Examine any commitments or promises you've made recently. Are they wise and aligned with God's will? If needed, adjust your approach to be more thoughtful and prayerful.

Day 4: The Cost of a Rash Decision

Scripture: *Judges 11:34-35 – "When Jephthah returned to his home in Mizpah, who should come out to meet him but his daughter, dancing to the sound of timbrels! She was an only child. Except for her, he had neither son nor daughter. When he saw her, he tore his clothes and cried, 'Oh no, my daughter! You have brought me down and I am devastated. I have made a vow to the LORD that I cannot break.'"*

Lesson: Jephthah's hasty vow cost him deeply. Instead of waiting on God's wisdom, he spoke without fully understanding the consequences.

Reflection: Are you making decisions based on emotion or desperation rather than seeking God's wisdom?

Challenge: Before making any significant decision today, pause and pray. Ask for wisdom and clarity rather than acting on impulse.

Day 5: Remembered for Both Strength and Weakness

Scripture: *Hebrews 11:32 – "And what more shall I say? I do not have time to tell about Gideon, Barak, Samson and Jephthah, about David and Samuel and the prophets,"*

Lesson: Despite his mistakes, Jephthah is remembered in Hebrews 11 for his faith. His life reminds us that God can use imperfect people, but it also warns us of the cost of rash decisions.

Reflection: Are you leaving behind a legacy of faithfulness, or are your actions clouded by avoidable mistakes?

Challenge: Take a step today to strengthen your faith and decision-making. Seek wisdom in Scripture and counsel before making commitments that impact your future.

Final Summary: What Jephthah Teaches Us

- **Day 1:** Overcome rejection—don't let your past define your future.

- **Day 2:** Be prepared—your skills and calling will be needed in God's timing.

- **Day 3:** Be careful with your words—don't make hasty promises to God or others.

- **Day 4:** Seek wisdom before acting—think through the long-term consequences.

- **Day 5:** Leave a strong legacy—faithfulness matters, but so does wise decision-making.

Life Application: Which lesson spoke to you the most? How will you incorporate it in your life? Pray for wisdom like Solomon rather than rashness like Jephthah. Trust God completely without feeling the need to bargain with Him.

Chapter 17

Samson: Strength, Weakness, and Redemption

(Judges 13-16)

Day 1: The Gift of Strength and Purpose

Scripture: *Judges 13:5 – "You will become pregnant and have a son whose head is never to be touched by a razor because the boy is to be a Nazirite, dedicated to God from the womb. He will take the lead in delivering Israel from the hands of the Philistines."*

Lesson: Samson was born with a God-given purpose—to deliver Israel. He was gifted with supernatural strength, but his calling required obedience.

Reflection: What gifts and strengths has God given you? Are you using them for His purpose?

Challenge: Take time today to identify your unique gifts and talents. Ask God how He wants you to use them for His glory this week.

Day 2: The Danger of Uncontrolled Desires

Scripture: *Judges 14:3 – "But his father and mother replied, 'Isn't there an acceptable woman among your relatives or among all our people? Must you go to the uncircumcised Philistines to get a wife?' But Samson said to his father, 'Get her for me. She's the right one for me.'"*

Lesson: Samson's downfall began with his inability to control his desires. He ignored godly wisdom and pursued relationships that led to his ruin.

Reflection: Are there desires in your life that are leading you away from God's will?

Challenge: Examine an area of your life where desires might be controlling you. Commit to discipline and seek God's guidance in making wise choices.

Day 3: When Strength Becomes a Weakness

Scripture: *Judges 16:19 – "After putting him to sleep on her lap, she called for someone to shave off the seven braids of his hair, and so began to subdue him. And his strength left him."*

Lesson: Samson relied on his physical strength but ignored his spiritual weakness. He became careless with his calling and lost everything.

Reflection: Are you placing more trust in your own abilities than in God? Are there areas where you have become spiritually careless?

Challenge: Identify one area where you've been relying on yourself instead of God. Surrender it to Him today and seek His strength.

Day 4: The Consequences of a Wasted Calling

Scripture: *Judges 16:21 – "Then the Philistines seized him, gouged out his eyes, and took him down to Gaza. Binding him with bronze shackles, they set him to grinding grain in the prison."*

Lesson: Samson's disobedience led him to captivity. He lost his vision—physically and spiritually. Sin always has consequences.

Reflection: Have you experienced the consequences of past mistakes? How has God used them to teach you?

Challenge: If you are dealing with consequences from past actions, ask for God's mercy and wisdom. Choose to learn from your mistakes rather than repeat them.

Day 5: Redemption and a Second Chance

Scripture: *Judges 16:28 – "Then Samson prayed to the Lord, 'Sovereign Lord, remember me. Please, God, strengthen me just once more...'"*

Lesson: Though Samson failed, God still used him in the end. His final act destroyed Israel's enemies, proving that God can redeem anyone who turns back to Him.

Reflection: Do you believe that God can still use you despite your past failures? Have you fully surrendered your life to Him?

Challenge: If you've fallen, get back up. Ask God for forgiveness and another chance to walk in your calling.

Final Summary: What Samson Teaches Us

- **Day 1:** Recognize your God-given gifts and purpose.
- **Day 2:** Control your desires before they control you.
- **Day 3:** Don't rely on your own strength—seek God's power.
- **Day 4:** Understand that sin has consequences.
- **Day 5:** Trust in God's redemption—your story isn't over.

Life Application: Which lesson struck you the most? How can you carry it out moving forward? Pray for wisdom and discipline to avoid Samson's mistakes and embrace the second chances God offers.

Chapter 18

Boaz: A Life of Integrity, Kindness, and Redeeming Love

(Ruth 1-4)

Day 1: A Man of Character and Integrity

Scripture: *Ruth 2:1 – "Now Naomi had a relative on her husband's side, a man of standing from the clan of Elimelek, whose name was Boaz."*

Lesson: Boaz was described as a "man of standing," meaning he was known for his integrity, honor, and faithfulness. He lived a life that reflected godly character in both business and personal matters.

Reflection: Are you living in a way that reflects integrity and godly character in all areas of your life?

Challenge: Examine your daily actions—at work, in relationships, and in private. Ask God to strengthen your character and make you a person of honor and integrity.

Day 2: Kindness and Generosity Toward the Vulnerable

Scripture: *Ruth 2:8-9 – "So Boaz said to Ruth, 'My daughter, listen to me. Don't go and glean in another field and don't go away from here. Stay here with the women who work for me. Watch the field where the men are harvesting, and follow along after the women. I have told the men not to lay a hand on you. And whenever you are thirsty, go and get a drink from the water jars the men have filled.'"*

Lesson: Boaz showed kindness and generosity to Ruth, a foreign widow, providing for her and ensuring her safety. His actions reflected God's heart for the vulnerable.

Reflection: Are you actively looking for ways to bless and protect those who are in need?

Challenge: Find a way to show kindness today—whether through generosity, encouragement, or offering help to someone in need.

Day 3: Honoring God's Commands in Relationships

Scripture: *Ruth 3:10-11 – "'The Lord bless you, my daughter,' he replied. 'This kindness is greater than that which you showed earlier: You have not run after the younger men, whether rich or poor. And now, my daughter, don't be afraid. I will do for you all you ask. All the people of my town know that you are a woman of noble character.'"*

Lesson: Boaz honored Ruth's character and followed God's laws rather than taking advantage of the situation. He upheld integrity in relationships rather than acting on impulse.

Reflection: Are you honoring God in your relationships, choosing integrity over selfish desires?

Challenge: Commit to honoring God in your relationships today—whether in friendships, dating, marriage, or business partnerships.

Day 4: Acting as a Kinsman-Redeemer

Scripture: *Ruth 4:9-10 – "Then Boaz announced to the elders and all the people, 'Today you are witnesses that I have bought from Naomi all the property of Elimelek, Kilion and Mahlon. I have also acquired Ruth the Moabite, Mahlon's widow, as my wife, in order to maintain the name of the dead with his property, so that his name will not disappear from among his family or from his hometown. Today you are witnesses!'"*

Lesson: Boaz willingly stepped in as Ruth's kinsman-redeemer, fulfilling his duty and foreshadowing Jesus, our ultimate Redeemer. His selflessness ensured the protection and future of Ruth and Naomi.

Reflection: Are you willing to take responsibility and step in to help others, even when it requires personal sacrifice?

Challenge: Consider how you can be a "redeemer" in someone's life today—whether through encouragement, financial help, or standing in the gap for someone in need.

Day 5: Blessings of a Faithful Life

Scripture: *Ruth 4:13, 17 – "So Boaz took Ruth and she became his wife. When he made love to her, the Lord enabled her to conceive, and she gave birth to a son... And they named him Obed. He was the father of Jesse, the father of David."*

Lesson: Because of Boaz's faithfulness and integrity, he became part of God's greater plan—his son Obed was the grandfather of King David, leading to the lineage of Jesus Christ.

Reflection: Are you living in a way that leaves a legacy of faith and obedience?

Challenge: Think about the legacy you are leaving behind. Invest in someone's life today—whether through mentoring, encouragement, or faith-filled leadership.

Final Summary: What Boaz Teaches Us

- **Day 1:** Live with integrity—your reputation should reflect God's character.
- **Day 2:** Show kindness and generosity—care for the vulnerable.
- **Day 3:** Honor God in relationships—choose integrity over selfishness.
- **Day 4:** Be a redeemer—step in for others in times of need.
- **Day 5:** Leave a legacy—your faithfulness impacts future generations.

Life Application: Which lesson challenged you the most? How will you live it out? Pray for a heart like Boaz—one that reflects integrity, kindness, and a willingness to be used in God's redemptive plan.

Chapter 19

Eli: A Life of Leadership, Neglect, and God's Sovereignty

(I Samuel 1-4)

Day 1: Speaking Blessing

Scripture: *1 Samuel 1:17* – *"Eli answered, 'Go in peace, and may the God of Israel grant you what you have asked of him.'"*

Lesson: Eli served as the high priest and judge over Israel, overseeing worship and leading God's people. When he found a woman named Hannah crying out to the LORD in anguish in the temple, he spoke a blessing over her and interceded for her request with her.

Reflection: Are you using your roles of leadership (whether at home, work, or church) to create opportunities to speak blessing over other people? Do you look for opportunities to come alongside others when they are in distress or in need?

Challenge: Identify a way that you can come alongside someone in need today, whether in prayer, service, or speaking a blessing, and step in boldly to encourage them today.

Day 2: Failing to Discipline Those Under His Care

Scripture: *1 Samuel 3:13* – *"For I told him that I would judge his family forever because of the sin he knew about; his sons blasphemed God, and he failed to restrain them."*

Lesson: Eli's sons were corrupt, and although Eli rebuked them, he didn't take action to stop them. He allowed their sins to continue, which ultimately led to judgment on his household.

Reflection: Are you ignoring sin or issues in your life or those under your leadership, hoping they will fix themselves?

Challenge: If there is an area where God is calling you to correct, guide, or discipline, act today in love and obedience.

Day 3: Recognizing and Encouraging God's Call on Others

Scripture: *1 Samuel 3:8-9 – "…Then Eli realized that the Lord was calling the boy. So Eli told Samuel, 'Go and lie down, and if He calls you, say, "Speak, Lord, for Your servant is listening…"'"*

Lesson: Even though Eli had personal failures, he still guided young Samuel to recognize and respond to God's voice. This shows that God can use us to lead others, even when we have our own struggles.

Reflection: Are you encouraging and guiding others in their faith, helping them recognize God's voice?

Challenge: Speak words of encouragement today to someone younger in the faith. Help guide them to seek and hear from God.

Day 4: The Consequences of Ignoring God's Warnings

Scripture: *1 Samuel 2:30 – "Therefore the Lord, the God of Israel, declares: 'I promised that members of your family would minister before Me forever.' But now the Lord declares: 'Far be it from Me! Those who honor Me I will honor, but those who despise Me will be disdained.'"*

Lesson: God warned Eli multiple times about the sins of his household, but he did not take meaningful action. Eventually, God removed his family from the priesthood.

Reflection: Are you heeding God's warnings in your life, or are you ignoring conviction and continuing in compromise?

Challenge: If God has been convicting you about something, take it seriously. Repent, and take action to change today.

Day 5: Leaving Behind a Mixed Legacy

Scripture: *1 Samuel 4:18 – "When he mentioned the ark of God, Eli fell backward off his chair by the side of the gate. His neck was broken and he died, for he was an old man, and he was heavy. He had led Israel forty years."*

Lesson: Eli's leadership lasted for decades, but it ended in tragedy. He was faithful in some ways (guiding Samuel), yet careless in others (failing to discipline his sons). His legacy was a mixture of faithfulness and failure.

Reflection: What kind of legacy are you leaving behind? Are you being faithful in all areas, or are there parts of your life that need realignment with God?

Challenge: Reflect on your spiritual legacy today. Write down one step you can take to ensure that what you leave behind honors God fully.

Final Summary: What Eli Teaches Us

- **Day 1:** Speak blessing—look for opportunities to encourage others.
- **Day 2:** Confront sin—ignoring wrongdoing leads to consequences.
- **Day 3:** Mentor others—help guide them to hear from God.
- **Day 4:** Take God's warnings seriously—repent and correct your path.
- **Day 5:** Build a lasting legacy—faithfulness matters in all areas.

Life Application: Which lesson resonated with you the most? How will it affect your decisions moving forward? Pray for a heart that is not divided like Eli's—one that listens, obeys, and honors God fully.

Chapter 20

Samuel: A Life of Listening and Leading

(I Samuel 1-28)

Day 1: Learning to Hear God's Voice

Scripture: *1 Samuel 3:10 – "The Lord came and stood there, calling as at the other times, 'Samuel! Samuel!' Then Samuel said, 'Speak, for your servant is listening.'"*

Lesson: Samuel was young when he first heard God's voice. Unlike Eli's sons, who ignored God, Samuel chose to listen and obey.

Reflection: Do you take time to listen for God's voice, or are you too distracted? How do you respond when He calls you?

Challenge: Set aside 10 minutes today in silence to listen to God. Ask Him to speak to you about anything He has to say, and write down any thoughts, verses, or impressions He places on your heart.

Day 2: Obedience Over Popularity

Scripture: *1 Samuel 3:18 – "So Samuel told him everything, hiding nothing from him. Then Eli said, 'He is the Lord; let him do what is good in his eyes.'"*

Lesson: Samuel had to deliver a hard message of judgment to Eli. He didn't sugarcoat the truth or shy away from obedience, even when it was difficult.

Reflection: Do you obey God even when it's hard, or do you fear what others will think?

Challenge: If there's a truth you've been avoiding, commit to speaking it today with love and courage.

Day 3: Stop Mourning and Move Forward

Scripture: *1 Samuel 16:1* – *"The Lord said to Samuel, 'How long will you mourn for Saul since I have rejected him as king over Israel? Fill your horn with oil and be on your way...'"*

Lesson: When things don't go how we think they should, we can get stuck mourning the results rather than seeking God for what's next. It is healthy to grieve a loss initially, but don't stay there. God is never surprised by events, and He already has something new in mind.

Reflection: Are you mourning something from your past and allowing it to keep you from your future?

Challenge: Focus today on letting go of the disappointment of the past and seeking God for His plan now, trusting that He is good.

Day 4: Feeling Rejected

Scripture: *1 Samuel 8:7* – *"And the Lord told him: 'Listen to all that the people are saying to you; it is not you they have rejected, but they have rejected me as their king."*

Lesson: Israel demanded a king like other nations, rejecting God's leadership through Samuel. Samuel warned them, but they insisted. Samuel could have gotten stuck in rejection, but God helped him see a bigger picture.

Reflection: Are you seeking approval from the world or people in your life instead of from God? Do you sometimes see people and circumstances through a lens of rejection instead of the truth of the bigger picture from God?

Challenge: Identify one way you've been conforming to the world's standards instead of God's. Choose today to follow His way instead. If you have been offended or are carrying rejection, ask God to show you a different perspective that leads from rejection to truth.

Day 5: Finishing Well—Staying Faithful to the End

Scripture: *1 Samuel 12:23* – *"As for me, far be it from me that I should sin against the Lord by failing to pray for you. And I will teach you the way that is good and right."*

Lesson: Even after being rejected by Israel, Samuel remained faithful. He continued to pray and intercede for them, proving his loyalty to God and His people.

Reflection: Are you staying faithful to your calling as a son of God, even when others don't appreciate you?

Challenge: Commit to praying for someone today who has wronged you or doesn't acknowledge your efforts.

Final Summary: What Samuel Teaches Us

- **Day 1:** Take time to listen to God's voice.
- **Day 2:** Obey God, even when it's difficult.
- **Day 3:** Finish mourning in order to move forward.
- **Day 4:** Reject worldly influences and offenses—ask God for the big picture.
- **Day 5:** Stay faithful, even when others don't value it.

Life Application: Which of these lessons stands out to you the most? How will you apply it moving forward? Pray for a heart that listens to God, obeys without fear, and stays faithful to the end.

Chapter 21

Saul: The Dangers of Pride and Disobedience

(I Samuel 9-31; I Chronicles 9-10)

Day 1: Called but Not Prepared

Scripture: *1 Samuel 10:22 – "So they inquired further of the LORD, 'Has the man come here yet?' And the LORD said, 'Yes, he has hidden himself among the supplies.'"*

Lesson: Saul was chosen by God to be king, but he started out insecure and hesitant. His fear led him to hide instead of stepping boldly into his calling.

Reflection: Are you letting fear stop you from stepping into the calling God has for you? Do you trust that He will equip you?

Challenge: Take a step of faith today in an area where fear has been holding you back. Trust God's power over your own abilities.

Day 2: Impatience Leads to Disobedience

Scripture: *1 Samuel 13:13 – "You have done a foolish thing," Samuel said. "You have not kept the command the Lord your God gave you; if you had, He would have established your kingdom over Israel for all time."*

Lesson: Saul grew impatient and took matters into his own hands by offering a sacrifice that only Samuel was supposed to give. His impatience cost him God's favor.

Reflection: Are you trying to force things to happen instead of waiting on God? Where in your life do you need to be more patient?

Challenge: Choose to wait on God in a specific area today. Resist the urge to act impulsively—pray and trust His timing.

Day 3: Partial Obedience is Still Disobedience

Scripture: *1 Samuel 15:22* – *"...To obey is better than sacrifice, and to heed is better than the fat of rams."*

Lesson: Saul was commanded to destroy everything in battle, but he spared the best livestock and King Agag. He justified his actions, but God saw his partial obedience as disobedience.

Reflection: Are you obeying God completely, or are you justifying partial obedience? Are there areas in your life where you are compromising?

Challenge: Identify one area where you've been obeying God halfway. Commit to full obedience today.

Day 4: Jealousy and Comparison Lead to Destruction

Scripture: *1 Samuel 18:9* – *"And from that time on Saul kept a close eye on David."*

Lesson: Saul's jealousy of David consumed him. Instead of focusing on his own calling, he became obsessed with bringing David down, which led to his downfall.

Reflection: Are you comparing yourself to others instead of focusing on what God has given you? Is jealousy stealing your peace?

Challenge: Celebrate someone else's success today instead of comparing yourself. Focus on what God is doing in your own life and be thankful.

Day 5: Finishing Poorly—What Happens When We Turn From God

Scripture: *1 Samuel 28:6-7* – *"He inquired of the Lord, but the Lord did not answer him... Saul then said to his attendants, 'Find me a woman who is a medium, so I may go and inquire of her.'"*

Lesson: After years of disobedience, Saul no longer heard from God. Instead of repenting, he sought answers through a medium. His refusal to fully surrender to God led to his tragic end.

Reflection: Are you seeking God first in your decisions? Do you turn to other sources for guidance instead of trusting Him?

Challenge: Make a commitment to seek God's direction before making any decisions today. Pray and wait for His leading.

Final Summary: What Saul Teaches Us

- **Day 1:** Don't let fear stop you—step boldly into your calling.
- **Day 2:** Wait on God—impatience leads to mistakes.
- **Day 3:** Obey fully—partial obedience is still disobedience.
- **Day 4:** Avoid jealousy—comparison steals joy.
- **Day 5:** Seek God's direction—don't turn to other sources.

Life Application: Which lesson convicted you the most? How will you continue to carry it out? Pray for a heart that is fully surrendered to God, one that obeys, trusts, and seeks Him above all else.

Chapter 22

David: A Man After God's Own Heart

(I Samuel 16-II Samuel 24; I Kings 1-2; I Chronicles 11-29)

Day 1: God Looks at the Heart

Scripture: *1 Samuel 16:7* – *"But the LORD said to Samuel, 'Do not consider his appearance or his height, for I have rejected him. The LORD does not look at the things people look at. People look at the outward appearance, but the LORD looks at the heart.'"*

Lesson: David was overlooked by others but chosen by God because of his heart. God values character over status, strength, or appearance.

Reflection: Are you more concerned with how others see you or with how God sees your heart? What areas of your heart need to be surrendered to Him?

Challenge: Spend time today examining your heart. Ask God to show you where you need to grow in character, integrity, and faith.

Day 2: Facing Giants with Faith

Scripture: *1 Samuel 17:45* – *"David said to the Philistine, 'You come against me with sword and spear and javelin, but I come against you in the name of the LORD Almighty, the God of the armies of Israel, whom you have defied.'"*

Lesson: David didn't fear Goliath because his confidence was in God, not in his own strength. Faith in God allows us to overcome the impossible.

Reflection: What "giants" are you facing in your life right now? Are you trying to fight them in your own strength or trusting God?

Challenge: Write down one fear, struggle, or challenge you are facing. Pray and declare that God is greater than your giant. Take a step of faith today.

Day 3: Walking in Integrity

Scripture: *1 Samuel 24:6 – "He said to his men, 'The LORD forbid that I should do such a thing to my master, the LORD's anointed, or lay my hand on him; for he is the anointed of the LORD.'"*

Lesson: David had opportunities to kill King Saul, but he refused to take shortcuts to his destiny. He honored God by waiting on His timing.

Reflection: Are you tempted to take shortcuts in life instead of waiting on God's timing? Are you walking in integrity when no one is watching?

Challenge: Choose integrity over shortcuts today. If you're in a situation where you could compromise, decide to honor God instead.

Day 4: When We Fall, Repentance Matters

Scripture: *Psalm 51:10 – "Create in me a pure heart, O God, and renew a steadfast spirit within me."*

Lesson: David sinned greatly but repented sincerely. His willingness to turn back to God made him a man after God's own heart.

Reflection: Do you quickly repent when you mess up, or do you try to justify your actions? Is there an area in your life that you need to bring before God?

Challenge: Take time today to confess anything that has been keeping you from God. Ask Him to renew your heart and restore your relationship with Him.

Day 5: Leaving a Legacy of Worship and Leadership

Scripture: *2 Samuel 7:16 – "Your house and your kingdom will endure forever before me; your throne will be established forever."*

Lesson: Despite his failures, David's faithfulness to God resulted in an everlasting legacy. His life of worship, leadership, and devotion to God impacted generations.

Reflection: What kind of legacy are you building? Are you living in a way that impacts others for God's glory?

Challenge: Think of one way you can impact others for Christ today—whether through encouragement, leadership, or worship. Take action to build a godly legacy.

Final Summary: What David Teaches Us

- **Day 1:** God looks at the heart—develop your character.
- **Day 2:** Face your giants with faith—God is greater than your fears.
- **Day 3:** Walk in integrity—trust God's timing.
- **Day 4:** Repent quickly—God restores a humble heart.
- **Day 5:** Build a lasting legacy—live for God's glory.

Life Application: Which lesson struck you the most? How will you continue to incorporate it in your life? Pray for the strength to be a man after God's own heart—living with faith, integrity, and devotion.

Chapter 23

Solomon: Wisdom, Success, and the Dangers of Compromise

(I Kings 1-11; I Chronicles 29-II Chronicles 9; Proverbs; Ecclesiastes; Songs of Solomon)

Day 1: Seeking Wisdom Above All Else

Scripture: *1 Kings 3:9 – "So give your servant a discerning heart to govern your people and to distinguish between right and wrong. For who is able to govern this great people of yours?"*

Lesson: When given the chance to ask for anything, Solomon chose wisdom over wealth, power, or long life. His request pleased God, and he was blessed abundantly.

Reflection: Do you seek wisdom in your decisions, or do you rely on your own understanding?

Challenge: Pray and ask God for wisdom today, especially in an area where you need guidance. Read a passage from Proverbs and apply it.

Day 2: The Power of a Rightly Ordered Life

Scripture: *1 Kings 4:29 – "God gave Solomon wisdom and very great insight, and a breadth of understanding as measureless as the sand on the seashore."*

Lesson: Solomon's wisdom brought order, peace, and prosperity to Israel. When we prioritize God's wisdom, our lives align with His design.

Reflection: Is your life rightly ordered around God's wisdom, or are distractions and worldly desires taking priority?

Challenge: Evaluate your priorities today. Make one change that better aligns your time, energy, or finances with God's wisdom.

Day 3: Enjoying God's Blessings Without Forgetting Him

Scripture: *1 Kings 10:23-24 – "King Solomon was greater in riches and wisdom than all the other kings of the earth. The whole world sought audience with Solomon to hear the wisdom God had put in his heart."*

Lesson: Solomon's success and wealth were gifts from God. However, later in life, he let those blessings distract him from his devotion to God.

Reflection: Are you enjoying God's blessings with gratitude, or have you become more focused on the gifts than the Giver?

Challenge: Take a moment to thank God for His blessings. Ask Him to help you enjoy them without letting them replace your dependence on Him.

Day 4: The Danger of Compromise

Scripture: *1 Kings 11:4 – "As Solomon grew old, his wives turned his heart after other gods, and his heart was not fully devoted to the LORD his God, as the heart of David his father had been."*

Lesson: Solomon's downfall wasn't an instant failure—it was a slow drift. He allowed compromise in his relationships, and it led to idolatry.

Reflection: Are there small compromises in your life that could lead you away from God over time?

Challenge: Examine your life for any area where you're compromising your faith. Make a commitment today to correct it before it leads you further away from God.

Day 5: The True Meaning of Life

Scripture: *Ecclesiastes 12:13 – "Now all has been heard; here is the conclusion of the matter: Fear God and keep His commandments, for this is the duty of all mankind."*

Lesson: At the end of his life, Solomon realized that wisdom, wealth, and pleasure are meaningless without devotion to God. True purpose comes from loving and obeying Him.

Reflection: Are you chasing after temporary things, or are you building your life on what truly matters?

Challenge: Make a decision today to live with eternity in mind. Focus on what has lasting value—your faith, character, and relationships with God and others.

Final Summary: What Solomon Teaches Us

- **Day 1:** Seek wisdom above all else—it brings true success.
- **Day 2:** Align your life with God's wisdom—order brings peace.
- **Day 3:** Enjoy blessings without forgetting the Giver.
- **Day 4:** Beware of compromise—it leads to spiritual decline.
- **Day 5:** True meaning is found in loving and obeying God.

Life Application: Which of these lessons do you need to apply most? How will you live it out? Pray for wisdom, discipline, and devotion to stay faithful in both success and trials.

Chapter 24

Elijah: Bold Faith, Spiritual Battles, and God's Sustaining Power

(I Kings 17–II Kings 2)

Day 1: Boldness in Standing for Truth

Scripture: *1 Kings 18:21 – "Elijah went before the people and said, 'How long will you waver between two opinions? If the Lord is God, follow him; but if Baal is God, follow him.' But the people said nothing."*

Lesson: Elijah stood alone against the false prophets of Baal. He was not afraid to challenge idolatry, even when he was outnumbered.

Reflection: Are you bold in standing for truth, or do you hesitate because of fear of rejection?

Challenge: Speak up for what is right today, even if it's unpopular. Stand firm in your faith with confidence.

Day 2: Trusting God for Provision

Scripture: *1 Kings 17:6 – "The ravens brought him bread and meat in the morning and bread and meat in the evening, and he drank from the brook."*

Lesson: God sustained Elijah during a famine in a miraculous way, showing that He provides for those who trust Him.

Reflection: Are you trusting God for your needs, or are you relying on your own strength and resources?

Challenge: Give your worries about provision to God today. Trust Him with your needs and resist the urge to control everything.

Day 3: God's Power in Prayer

Scripture: *James 5:17-18 – "Elijah was a human being, even as we are. He prayed earnestly that it would not rain, and it did not rain on the land for three and a half years. Again he prayed, and the heavens gave rain..."*

Lesson: Elijah's prayers changed the course of nature, proving that a single person's faith-filled prayer can bring powerful results.

Reflection: Do you believe in the power of prayer? Are you praying with faith, or just out of routine?

Challenge: Pray boldly today for something impossible. Trust that God hears and answers prayers according to His will.

Day 4: When Faith Feels Weak

Scripture: *1 Kings 19:4 – "...He came to a broom bush, sat down under it and prayed that he might die. 'I have had enough, LORD,' he said. 'Take my life; I am no better than my ancestors.'"*

Lesson: Even after great victories, Elijah faced deep discouragement and exhaustion. Yet God met him with compassion, not condemnation.

Reflection: Do you ever feel burned out or discouraged in your faith journey? How do you handle those moments?

Challenge: If you're feeling weary, take time today to rest and reconnect with God. Let Him restore your strength.

Day 5: Hearing God in the Quiet

Scripture: *1 Kings 19:12-13 – "...after the fire came a gentle whisper. When Elijah heard it, he pulled his cloak over his face..."*

Lesson: God didn't speak to Elijah in dramatic ways, but in a quiet whisper. Sometimes, we need to slow down to truly hear Him.

Reflection: Are you making space in your life to hear God's voice, or are you too busy and distracted?

Challenge: Set aside quiet time today with no distractions. Listen for God's voice through Scripture, prayer, and stillness.

Final Summary: What Elijah Teaches Us

- **Day 1:** Be bold in standing for truth.
- **Day 2:** Trust God for your provision—He will sustain you.
- **Day 3:** Pray with faith—prayer changes things.
- **Day 4:** Even strong believers get discouraged—seek God's restoration.
- **Day 5:** God often speaks in the quiet—make space to hear Him.

Life Application: Which of these lessons do you need to practice most? How will you let it affect your decisions moving forward? Pray for courage, trust, and a deep awareness of God's presence in your life.

Chapter 25

King Ahab: Compromise, Idolatry, and Missed Opportunities

(I Kings 16-22; II Kings 10; II Chronicles 18)

Day 1: Choosing the Wrong Influences

Scripture: *1 Kings 16:30-31* – *"Ahab son of Omri did more evil in the eyes of the Lord than any of those before him. He not only considered it trivial to commit the sins of Jeroboam son of Nebat, but he also married Jezebel daughter of Ethbaal king of the Sidonians, and began to serve Baal and worship him."*

Lesson: Ahab's downfall began with choosing the wrong influences. His marriage to Jezebel led him into deeper sin and idolatry, showing that who we align ourselves with greatly affects our faith.

Reflection: Are there people or influences in your life leading you away from God's truth?

Challenge: Evaluate your closest relationships today. Ask God for wisdom to surround yourself with influences that encourage your faith.

Day 2: The Danger of Idolatry and Spiritual Compromise

Scripture: *1 Kings 18:18* – *"'I have not made trouble for Israel,' Elijah replied. 'But you and your father's family have. You have abandoned the Lord's commands and have followed the Baals.'"*

Lesson: Ahab allowed idol worship to flourish in Israel. His compromise didn't just affect him—it brought destruction to his nation. Turning away from God leads to spiritual ruin.

Reflection: Are you compromising your faith by allowing things in your life that compete with God?

Challenge: Identify and remove anything that is taking God's place in your life today—whether it's money, status, entertainment, or relationships.

Day 3: Ignoring God's Warnings

Scripture: *1 Kings 21:20 – "Ahab said to Elijah, 'So you have found me, my enemy!' 'I have found you,' he answered, 'because you have sold yourself to do evil in the eyes of the LORD.'"*

Lesson: God repeatedly sent warnings through Elijah, but Ahab treated Elijah as an enemy instead of listening. Ignoring God's warnings leads to judgment.

Reflection: Are you resisting God's correction in any area of your life?

Challenge: Humbly ask God today to reveal any warnings He is giving you, and respond with repentance instead of resistance.

Day 4: Temporary Repentance, But No True Change

Scripture: *1 Kings 21:27-29 – "When Ahab heard these words, he tore his clothes, put on sackcloth and fasted. He lay in sackcloth and went around meekly. Then the word of the Lord came to Elijah… 'Have you noticed how Ahab has humbled himself before Me? Because he has humbled himself, I will not bring this disaster in his day…'"*

Lesson: Ahab showed outward humility, but his heart didn't truly change. Temporary remorse is not the same as lasting repentance.

Reflection: Is your repentance genuine, leading to real change, or is it just temporary remorse?

Challenge: If there's an area where you've been repeating the same mistakes, seek true repentance today. Ask God for the strength to change.

Day 5: Facing the Consequences of Disobedience

Scripture: *1 Kings 22:37-38 – "So the king died and was brought to Samaria, and they buried him there. They washed the chariot at a pool in Samaria (where the prostitutes bathed), and the dogs licked up his blood, as the word of the LORD had declared."*

Lesson: Ahab refused to fully obey God, and his life ended in judgment. Ignoring God's commands leads to painful consequences, not just for us but for those around us.

Reflection: Are you taking God's commands seriously, or are you treating them lightly like Ahab did?

Challenge: Examine your obedience to God today. If there's anything you need to correct, take action immediately rather than delaying.

Final Summary: What King Ahab Teaches Us

- **Day 1:** Choose godly influences—don't let relationships lead you away from God.
- **Day 2:** Avoid spiritual compromise—don't allow idols to take God's place.
- **Day 3:** Listen to God's warnings—ignoring them leads to destruction.
- **Day 4:** Repent with sincerity—remorse isn't enough; true change is needed.
- **Day 5:** Obey God fully—disobedience has lasting consequences.

Life Application: Which lesson spoke to you the most? What will you do to apply it moving forward? Pray for a heart that listens to God, repents sincerely, and follows Him fully.

Chapter 26

King Jehoshaphat: A Life of Seeking God, Bold Faith, and Wise Leadership

(I Kings 15,22; II Kings 3,8; II Chronicles 17-21)

Day 1: Seeking God First in Every Decision

Scripture: *2 Chronicles 17:3-4 – "The LORD was with Jehoshaphat because he followed the ways of his father David before him. He did not consult the Baals but sought the God of his father and followed His commands rather than the practices of Israel."*

Lesson: Jehoshaphat made it a priority to seek God in every decision. Instead of following the ways of the world, he followed God's commands, which brought blessings and protection.

Reflection: Are you seeking God first in your decisions, or are you relying on worldly wisdom and personal desires?

Challenge: Commit today to pray and seek God's guidance before making any major decisions. Ask Him for wisdom and direction.

Day 2: Teaching and Spreading God's Word

Scripture: *2 Chronicles 17:9 – "They taught throughout Judah, taking with them the Book of the Law of the Lord; they went around to all the towns of Judah and taught the people."*

Lesson: Jehoshaphat prioritized teaching God's Word to his people. He knew that a nation grounded in Scripture would be strong and blessed.

Reflection: Are you investing time in learning and sharing God's Word with others?

Challenge: Make time today to study Scripture and share something you've learned with a friend, family member, or colleague.

Day 3: The Danger of Wrong Alliances

Scripture: *2 Chronicles 18:1 – "Now Jehoshaphat had great wealth and honor, and he allied himself with Ahab by marriage."*

Lesson: Although Jehoshaphat was a godly king, he made an alliance with Ahab, one of Israel's most wicked rulers. This partnership led to unnecessary trouble and almost cost him his life.

Reflection: Are there partnerships, relationships, or agreements in your life that are pulling you away from God?

Challenge: Examine your relationships today. Ask God if there are any alliances you need to break or realign for His glory.

Day 4: Trusting God in the Face of Battle

Scripture: *2 Chronicles 20:12 – "Our God, will You not judge them? For we have no power to face this vast army that is attacking us. We do not know what to do, but our eyes are on You."*

Lesson: When faced with a massive enemy attack, Jehoshaphat didn't panic—he prayed. He acknowledged his own weakness and relied completely on God's power.

Reflection: When challenges come, do you first panic or first pray?

Challenge: If you're facing a problem today, pause and pray before taking any action. Put your trust in God's strength, not your own.

Day 5: Victory Through Worship and Faith

Scripture: *2 Chronicles 20:22 – "As they began to sing and praise, the Lord set ambushes against the men of Ammon and Moab and Mount Seir who were invading Judah, and they were defeated."*

Lesson: Jehoshaphat led his army into battle with worship instead of weapons. God responded to their faith by giving them victory without them having to fight.

Reflection: Are you using worship and faith as spiritual weapons in your battles, or are you relying only on human strength?

Challenge: Spend time today worshiping and praising God, even before you see the answer to your prayers. Declare victory in faith!

Final Summary: What King Jehoshaphat Teaches Us

- **Day 1:** Seek God first—His wisdom is greater than any human advice.
- **Day 2:** Prioritize God's Word—learn it, live it, and teach it to others.
- **Day 3:** Avoid wrong alliances—choose relationships that honor God.
- **Day 4:** Trust God in crisis—turn to Him in prayer rather than fearing.
- **Day 5:** Worship as a weapon—praise God even before the battle is won.

Life Application: Which lesson stood out to you the most? How will you continue to carry it out? Pray for a heart like Jehoshaphat's—one that seeks God first, trusts Him in battles, and praises Him in all circumstances.

Chapter 27

Elisha: A Life of Faith, Miracles, and Service

(I Kings 19-21; II Kings 1-13)

Day 1: Answering God's Call with Boldness

Scripture: *1 Kings 19:19-21* – *"…Elijah went up to him and threw his cloak around him… So Elisha left him and went back. He took his yoke of oxen and slaughtered them… Then he set out to follow Elijah and became his servant."*

Lesson: Elisha immediately left everything to follow God's calling. He slaughtered his oxen and burned his plow, showing that there was no turning back.

Reflection: Are you willing to leave behind comfort and security to follow God's calling on your life, or do you have a plan B (keeping the oxen alive, just in case)?

Challenge: Identify something that is holding you back from fully committing to God's purpose. Take a step today to let it go.

Day 2: Asking for More of God

Scripture: *2 Kings 2:9* – *"…Elijah said to Elisha, 'Tell me, what can I do for you'…'Let me inherit a double portion of your spirit,' Elisha replied."*

Lesson: Elisha was not content with a small calling—he boldly asked for a greater portion of God's power and anointing.

Reflection: Do you pray bold prayers, asking God to use you in greater ways?

Challenge: Ask God today for greater faith, wisdom, or boldness to do His work. Step out in faith and believe that He will equip you.

Day 3: Seeing with Spiritual Eyes

Scripture: *2 Kings 6:16-17* – *"'Don't be afraid,' the prophet answered. 'Those who are with us are more than those who are with them.' And Elisha prayed, 'Open his eyes, LORD, so that he may see.' Then the LORD opened the servant's eyes, and he looked and saw the hills full of horses and chariots of fire all around Elisha."*

Lesson: Elisha's servant saw danger, but Elisha saw God's unseen protection. Faith allows us to see beyond our circumstances.

Reflection: Are you looking at your problems through fear or faith?

Challenge: Choose to see your challenges through God's promises instead of fear. Declare a promise from Scripture over your life or a difficult situation today.

Day 4: Serving Others Through Miracles

Scripture: *2 Kings 6:5-7* – *"As one of them was cutting down a tree, the ax head fell into the water. He cried out, 'Oh no, master! It was borrowed!'...When he showed Elisha the place, Elisha cut off a piece of wood. He threw it into the water at that place and made the ax head float. Elisha said, 'Pick it up.'..."*

Lesson: Elisha performed miracles to bless others—causing borrowed ax heads to float, multiplying food, healing the sick, and even raising the dead. His life was marked by service.

Reflection: Are you using your gifts and resources to serve others, or are you more focused on yourself?

Challenge: Find one way to serve someone today —through encouragement, generosity, time, or prayer.

Day 5: Leaving a Lasting Legacy

Scripture: *2 Kings 13:21* – *"Once while some Israelites were burying a man, suddenly they saw a band of raiders; so they threw the man's body into Elisha's tomb. When the body touched Elisha's bones, the man came to life and stood up on his feet."*

Lesson: Even after his death, Elisha's life carried power. His faith left a legacy that impacted generations.

Reflection: What kind of spiritual legacy are you leaving behind? How will others be influenced by your faith?

Challenge: Do something today that will have lasting spiritual impact—mentor someone, pray for someone, or share your testimony.

Final Summary: What Elisha Teaches Us

- **Day 1:** Fully commit to God's calling—leave behind distractions and Plan B's.
- **Day 2:** Ask boldly for more of God's power.
- **Day 3:** See challenges through faith, not fear.
- **Day 4:** Use your gifts to serve others.
- **Day 5:** Live in a way that leaves a lasting legacy of faith.

Life Application: Which lesson do you need to apply the most? How will you live it out moving forward? Pray for boldness, faith, and a servant's heart, and ask God to use you for His glory.

Chapter 28

Gehazi (Elisha's Servant): A Journey of Fear, Faith, and Spiritual Vision

(II Kings 1-8)

Day 1: Serving but Struggling with Faith

Scripture: *2 Kings 4:42-44 – "A man came from Baal Shalishah, bringing the man of God twenty loaves of barley bread… 'How can I set this before a hundred men?' his servant asked. But Elisha answered, 'Give it to the people to eat, for this is what the Lord says: They will eat and have some left over.' Then he set it before them, and they ate and had some left over, according to the word of the Lord."*

Lesson: Elisha's servant witnessed miracles firsthand, yet he doubted God's ability to provide. Sometimes, even when we serve God closely, we struggle to trust Him fully.

Reflection: Are you serving God but still doubting His ability to provide and perform miracles in your life?

Challenge: Surrender your doubts to God today. Ask Him to strengthen your faith and help you trust in His provision.

Day 2: Focusing on the Problem Instead of God's Power

Scripture: *2 Kings 6:15 – "When the servant of the man of God got up and went out early the next morning, an army with horses and chariots had surrounded the city. 'Oh no, my lord! What shall we do?' the servant asked."*

Lesson: Elisha's servant panicked when he saw the enemy surrounding them. His fear came from focusing on the visible problem instead of trusting in the unseen power of God.

Reflection: Are you more focused on the challenges in front of you than on the power of God behind you?

Challenge: Shift your perspective today. Instead of focusing on your problems, pray and declare God's power over your situation.

Day 3: Seeing with Spiritual Eyes

Scripture: *2 Kings 6:16-17 – "'Don't be afraid,' the prophet answered. 'Those who are with us are more than those who are with them.' And Elisha prayed, 'Open his eyes, Lord, so that he may see.' Then the Lord opened the servant's eyes, and he looked and saw the hills full of horses and chariots of fire all around Elisha."*

Lesson: The servant's fear was replaced by faith when his spiritual eyes were opened. Sometimes, we need God to open our eyes to see His protection, provision, and power.

Reflection: Are you relying only on what you see in the natural, or are you asking God for spiritual vision?

Challenge: Pray today for God to open your spiritual eyes. Ask Him to help you see beyond your circumstances to His greater plan.

Day 4: Learning to Rely on God's Miraculous Power

Scripture: *2 Kings 4:14-16 – "'What can be done for her?' Elisha asked. Gehazi said, 'She has no son, and her husband is old.' Then Elisha said, 'Call her.' So he called her, and she stood in the doorway. 'About this time next year,' Elisha said, 'you will hold a son in your arms...'"*

Lesson: Elisha's servant saw many miracles take place for others, yet he often failed to believe in the miraculous for himself. Believing God can move isn't enough—we must believe it for our own lives.

Reflection: Are you trusting in God's miraculous power for your own life, or just recognizing it in others?

Challenge: Pray in faith for a miracle in your life today. Trust that God is still working in miraculous ways.

Day 5: The Danger of Greed and Dishonesty (Gehazi's Mistake)

Scripture: *2 Kings 5:20 – "Gehazi, the servant of Elisha, the man of God, said to himself, 'My master was too easy on Naaman... I will run after him and get something from him.'"*

Lesson: Gehazi, Elisha's servant, allowed greed and deception to ruin his life. Instead of learning faith and integrity from Elisha, he sought personal gain and suffered the consequences.

Reflection: Are you allowing greed, dishonesty, or selfish ambition to pull you away from God's calling?

Challenge: Examine your heart today. If there is any area of dishonesty or greed, confess it and realign your desires with God's will.

Final Summary: What Elisha's Servant Teaches Us

- **Day 1:** Trust God's provision—don't let doubt keep you from seeing His miracles.

- **Day 2:** Shift your focus—look at God's power, not just the problems around you.

- **Day 3:** Pray for spiritual vision—ask God to help you see with faith.

- **Day 4:** Believe in God's miracles—trust that He works in your life, not just in others.

- **Day 5:** Guard against greed and dishonesty—stay faithful in your calling.

Life Application: Which lesson convicted you the most? How will you incorporate it in your daily life? Pray for a heart like Elisha's servant should have had—one that sees God's power, trusts His provision, and remains faithful in integrity.

Chapter 29

Naaman: A Journey of Pride, Humility, and God's Healing Power

(II Kings 5)

Day 1: The Limits of Power and Success

Scripture: *2 Kings 5:1 – "Now Naaman was commander of the army of the king of Aram. He was a great man in the sight of his master and highly regarded, because through him the Lord had given victory to Aram. He was a valiant soldier, but he had leprosy."*

Lesson: Naaman was a powerful and successful leader, but his status couldn't save him from his condition. His story reminds us that no matter how high we rise, we all have weaknesses and need God.

Reflection: Are you relying on your own strength and achievements, or do you recognize your need for God's power and healing?

Challenge: Acknowledge an area in your life where you need God's help today. Surrender it to Him in prayer, trusting that His power is greater than your own.

Day 2: God Works Through Unexpected Messengers

Scripture: *2 Kings 5:2-3 – "Now bands of raiders from Aram had gone out and had taken captive a young girl from Israel, and she served Naaman's wife. She said to her mistress, 'If only my master would see the prophet who is in Samaria! He would cure him of his leprosy.'"*

Lesson: God used a humble, captive servant girl to point Naaman toward healing. Sometimes, divine guidance comes from the least expected sources.

Reflection: Are you open to God speaking to you through unexpected people and circumstances?

Challenge: Pay attention today to wisdom and guidance from unexpected places—whether from a child, a coworker, or a situation that challenges you.

Day 3: Humbling Ourselves to Obey God's Instructions

Scripture: *2 Kings 5:10-11 – "Elisha sent a messenger to say to him, 'Go, wash yourself seven times in the Jordan, and your flesh will be restored and you will be cleansed.' But Naaman went away angry and said, 'I thought that he would surely come out to me and stand and call on the name of the Lord his God, wave his hand over the spot and cure me of my leprosy.'"*

Lesson: Naaman expected a grand, dramatic miracle, but God's instructions were simple. Naaman's pride almost prevented his healing. Often, obedience requires humility.

Reflection: Are you rejecting God's direction because it seems too simple, too ordinary, or not what you expected?

Challenge: Ask God to show you any area where pride or stubbornness is stopping you from obeying Him. Choose to follow His way, even when it doesn't make sense to you.

Day 4: The Power of Simple Obedience

Scripture: *2 Kings 5:14 – "So he went down and dipped himself in the Jordan seven times, as the man of God had told him, and his flesh was restored and became clean like that of a young boy."*

Lesson: When Naaman humbled himself and obeyed, he was healed. His story reminds us that God's promises are often just waiting for our obedience. We get to choose whether to claim God's promises or not when we choose whether to submit to His authority or not.

Reflection: Is there an area of your life where you are not submitting to God's authority and being obedient? What promises of God might you be missing out on because of disobedience?

Challenge: Ask for forgiveness today for an area where you have not been submitting to God's authority. Take an active step toward submitting to His authority and ask God for His blessing to be reestablished in that part of your life.

Day 5: A Changed Heart and True Worship

Scripture: *2 Kings 5:15 – "Then Naaman and all his attendants went back to the man of God. He stood before him and said, 'Now I know that there is no God in all the world except in Israel...'"*

Lesson: Naaman didn't just receive physical healing—his heart was changed. He recognized the power of the one true God and committed himself to worshiping Him.

Reflection: Has God changed your heart through His work in your life? Are you giving Him full credit for what He has done?

Challenge: Spend time today thanking God for the ways He has worked in your life. Worship Him with a heart of gratitude and renewed faith.

Final Summary: What Naaman Teaches Us

- **Day 1:** Success can't replace our need for God—humble yourself before Him.
- **Day 2:** God speaks through unexpected messengers—listen for His voice.
- **Day 3:** Obedience requires humility—don't let pride keep you from God's blessings.
- **Day 4:** God's promises are for those who are living under His authority—submit to Him.
- **Day 5:** God's power leads to true worship—give Him glory for His work in your life.

Life Application: Which lesson resonated with you the most? How will you let it affect your decisions moving forward? Pray for a heart like Naaman's after his healing—one that listens, obeys, and gives God the glory.

Chapter 30

King Hezekiah: A Life of Faith, Prayer, and Renewal

(II Kings 18-20; II Chronicles 29-32; Isaiah 38-39)

Day 1: Trusting God in Uncertain Times

Scripture: *2 Kings 18:5-6 – "Hezekiah trusted in the LORD, the God of Israel. There was no one like him among all the kings of Judah, either before him or after him. He held fast to the LORD and did not stop following Him; he kept the commands the LORD had given Moses."*

Lesson: Hezekiah's reign was marked by unwavering trust in God. He didn't rely on alliances or personal strength but fully depended on God's guidance and power.

Reflection: Are you trusting God completely in your life, or are you relying on human solutions?

Challenge: Surrender a situation to God today that you've been trying to control on your own. Choose to trust Him fully.

Day 2: Restoring True Worship and Removing Idolatry

Scripture: *2 Chronicles 29:3-5 – "In the first month of the first year of his reign, he opened the doors of the temple of the Lord and repaired them. He brought in the priests and the Levites, assembled them in the square on the east side and said: 'Listen to me, Levites! Consecrate yourselves now and consecrate the temple of the Lord, the God of your ancestors. Remove all defilement from the sanctuary.'"*

Lesson: Hezekiah prioritized restoring true worship and removing everything that dishonored God. He understood that revival starts with personal and corporate renewal.

Reflection: Is there anything in your life that is crowding out your worship and devotion to God?

Challenge: Identify and remove one distraction or habit that is keeping you from fully worshiping and seeking God.

Day 3: Turning to God in Crisis

Scripture: *2 Kings 19:14-15 – "Hezekiah received the letter from the messengers and read it. Then he went up to the temple of the LORD and spread it out before the LORD. And Hezekiah prayed to the LORD: 'LORD, the God of Israel, enthroned between the cherubim, You alone are God over all the kingdoms of the earth. You have made heaven and earth.'"*

Lesson: When threatened by the Assyrian king Sennacherib, Hezekiah didn't panic—he prayed. Instead of relying on his own strategy, he laid his concerns before God.

Reflection: Do you turn to God first in a crisis, or do you try to handle it on your own?

Challenge: Bring your burdens to God in prayer today. Write them down, lay them before Him, and trust in His answer.

Day 4: Experiencing God's Power and Deliverance

Scripture: *2 Kings 19:35 – "That night the angel of the LORD went out and put to death a hundred and eighty-five thousand in the Assyrian camp. When the people got up the next morning—there were all the dead bodies!"*

Lesson: God responded to Hezekiah's faith by delivering Judah miraculously. He fights for those who trust Him and remain obedient to His word.

Reflection: Are you believing in God's power to deliver and fight for you, or are you trying to solve everything in your own strength?

Challenge: Declare victory in an area of your life where you need God's intervention. Trust that He is working even if you don't see the results yet.

Day 5: The Danger of Pride After Success

Scripture: *2 Chronicles 32:25* – *"But Hezekiah's heart was proud and he did not respond to the kindness shown him; therefore the LORD's wrath was on him and on Judah and Jerusalem."*

Lesson: Despite his faithfulness, Hezekiah struggled with pride after God blessed him. Success can lead to arrogance if we forget that all victories come from God.

Reflection: Are you staying humble and giving God credit for your successes, or are you taking the glory for yourself?

Challenge: Take time today to thank God for His blessings. Acknowledge that all good things come from Him and ask Him to guard you against pride.

Final Summary: What King Hezekiah Teaches Us

- **Day 1:** Trust God completely—He is greater than any challenge.
- **Day 2:** Remove spiritual distractions—restore true worship in your life.
- **Day 3:** Bring your problems to God first—prayer is the most powerful weapon.
- **Day 4:** Believe in God's deliverance—He fights for those who trust Him.
- **Day 5:** Stay humble—success should lead to gratitude, not pride.

Life Application: Which lesson do you most need to practice? How will you let it affect your decisions moving forward? Pray for a heart that trusts in God, leads in faithfulness, and remains humble in success.

Chapter 31

King Josiah: A Life of Spiritual Revival, Obedience, and Seeking God's Truth

(II Kings 22-23; II Chronicles 34-35)

Day 1: Seeking God from a Young Age

Scripture: *2 Chronicles 34:1-3 – "Josiah was eight years old when he became king, and he reigned in Jerusalem thirty-one years. He did what was right in the eyes of the LORD and followed the ways of his father David, not turning aside to the right or to the left. In the eighth year of his reign, while he was still young, he began to seek the God of his father David..."*

Lesson: Josiah didn't wait until he was older to seek God—he pursued Him at a young age. His early commitment to God set the foundation for his righteous reign.

Reflection: Are you seeking God daily, no matter your stage in life?

Challenge: Make it a priority today to spend intentional time in prayer and Bible study, seeking God with a whole heart.

Day 2: Removing Idols and Purifying Worship

Scripture: *2 Chronicles 34:4 – "Under his direction the altars of the Baals were torn down; he cut to pieces the incense altars that were above them and smashed the Asherah poles and the idols..."*

Lesson: Josiah actively removed anything that dishonored God. He didn't just acknowledge sin—he destroyed every trace of it. True worship requires a clean heart and undivided devotion.

Reflection: Are there any "idols" or distractions in your life that are competing with your devotion to God?

Challenge: Identify one thing that is taking too much of your focus away from God and commit to removing or reducing it today.

Day 3: Rediscovering and Obeying God's Word

Scripture: *2 Chronicles 34:14-15 – "While they were bringing out the money that had been taken into the temple of the LORD, Hilkiah the priest found the Book of the Law of the LORD that had been given through Moses. Hilkiah said to Shaphan the secretary, 'I have found the Book of the Law in the temple of the LORD...'"*

Lesson: God's Word had been lost and forgotten, but when it was rediscovered during Josiah's reign, Josiah took it very seriously. Instead of ignoring it, he responded with obedience and humility and made sure the Word was read to the people. The Bible must be at the center of true revival.

Reflection: Are you regularly reading and applying God's Word, or have you neglected it in certain areas of your life?

Challenge: Commit to daily Bible reading and reflection. Choose a passage today and ask God how you can apply it to your life.

Day 4: Responding to God with a Tender Heart

Scripture: *2 Chronicles 34:27 – "Because your heart was responsive and you humbled yourself before God when you heard what He spoke against this place and its people... and you wept in My presence, I have heard you, declares the Lord."*

Lesson: Josiah had a tender, humble heart. When he heard God's warnings, he didn't react with pride or resistance—he repented and sought God's mercy. A teachable heart allows God to work powerfully in our lives.

Reflection: Are you humble and responsive to God's correction, or do you resist change?

Challenge: Ask God to soften your heart today. If there's an area where you need to change, respond with humility and obedience.

Day 5: Leading Others to Spiritual Renewal

Scripture: *2 Chronicles 34:31-32 – "The king stood by his pillar and renewed the covenant in the presence of the LORD—to follow the LORD and keep His commands... with all his heart and all his soul... Then he had everyone in Jerusalem and Benjamin pledge themselves to it..."*

Lesson: Josiah didn't just change his own life—he led his entire nation into revival. True leaders influence others toward righteousness.

Reflection: Are you encouraging others to grow spiritually, or are you only focusing on your own walk with God?

Challenge: Take one step today to encourage someone in their faith—whether through prayer, sharing Scripture, or leading by example.

Final Summary: What King Josiah Teaches Us

- **Day 1:** Seek God wholeheartedly—don't wait to pursue Him.
- **Day 2:** Remove idols—get rid of anything competing with God in your life.
- **Day 3:** Rediscover and obey God's Word—true revival starts with Scripture.
- **Day 4:** Respond with humility—let God's correction lead you to transformation.
- **Day 5:** Lead others to God—encourage spiritual renewal in those around you.

Life Application: Which lesson challenged you the most? How will you carry it out moving forward? Pray for a heart like Josiah's—one that seeks God earnestly, removes distractions, obeys His Word, and leads others to Him.

Chapter 32

Job: Enduring Suffering with Faith and Trust

(Job)

Day 1: Trusting God Even When Life Falls Apart

Scripture: *Job 1:21 – "...The LORD gave and the LORD has taken away; may the name of the LORD be praised."*

Lesson: Job lost everything—his wealth, children, and health—yet he still praised God. His faith was not based on circumstances but on God's sovereignty.

Reflection: Do you trust God even when life doesn't make sense? Is your faith dependent on blessings, or is it rooted in who God is?

Challenge: Take a moment today to thank God, not just for your blessings but for who He is, even in difficult times.

Day 2: Holding Onto Integrity in the Storm

Scripture: *Job 2:9-10 – "His wife said to him, 'Are you still maintaining your integrity? Curse God and die!' He replied...'Shall we accept good from God, and not trouble?' In all this, Job did not sin in what he said."*

Lesson: Even when those around him doubted, Job refused to turn away from God. He chose integrity over bitterness.

Reflection: Are you staying faithful in trials, or are you allowing difficulties to weaken your commitment to God?

Challenge: Examine your heart today. If you're struggling with doubt or bitterness, bring it to God in honest prayer.

Day 3: Seeking God Instead of Easy Answers

Scripture: *Job 13:15 – "Though he slay me, yet will I hope in him..."*

Lesson: Job's friends offered explanations, but Job sought God Himself. He didn't just want reasons—he wanted a deeper relationship with God.

Reflection: When facing trials, do you seek quick answers, or do you press deeper into your relationship with God?

Challenge: Spend time today in prayer, not asking "why" but seeking God's presence in your situation.

Day 4: God's Wisdom is Greater Than Ours

Scripture: *Job 38:4 – "Where were you when I laid the earth's foundation? Tell me, if you understand."*

Lesson: God reminded Job that His ways are beyond human understanding. Instead of answering Job's questions, He revealed His power and wisdom.

Reflection: Are you willing to trust God's wisdom even when you don't understand what He's doing?

Challenge: Surrender a situation in your life today where you've been demanding answers. Trust God's wisdom over your own.

Day 5: Restoration Comes in God's Timing

Scripture: *Job 42:10 – "After Job had prayed for his friends, the LORD restored his fortunes and gave him twice as much as he had before."*

Lesson: Job's suffering was not the end of his story. God restored him, but only after Job prayed for those who had hurt him. Restoration often comes through forgiveness and renewed faith.

Reflection: Are you holding onto pain or resentment that might be blocking God's restoration in your life?

Challenge: Pray for someone who has wronged you and forgive them. Release any bitterness and trust God to restore what was lost in His perfect timing.

Final Summary: What Job Teaches Us

- **Day 1:** Trust God even when life falls apart.
- **Day 2:** Stay faithful in trials—don't let hardship shake your integrity.
- **Day 3:** Seek God, not just answers—His presence is greater than explanations.
- **Day 4:** God's wisdom is beyond our understanding—trust Him fully.
- **Day 5:** Restoration comes through faith, patience, and forgiveness.

Life Application: Which lesson resonates most with you? How will you continue to apply it in your life? Pray for the strength to endure trials with faith, trust God's wisdom, and believe in His restoration.

Chapter 33

Isaiah: A Life of Calling, Conviction, and Prophetic Vision

(Isaiah)

Day 1: Responding to God's Call

Scripture: *Isaiah 6:8 – "Then I heard the voice of the Lord saying, 'Whom shall I send? And who will go for us?' And I said, 'Here am I. Send me!'"*

Lesson: Isaiah willingly accepted God's call without hesitation. He didn't ask for details—he simply said, "Send me."

Reflection: Are you open to God's call in your life, even if it's uncertain? Do you hesitate or resist when God calls you?

Challenge: Pray today and tell God, "Here I am, send me." Be open to how He may use you in small or big ways.

Day 2: God's Holiness and Our Need for Cleansing

Scripture: *Isaiah 6:5-7 – "'Woe to me!' I cried. 'I am ruined! For I am a man of unclean lips... and my eyes have seen the King, the LORD Almighty.' Then one of the seraphim flew to me with a live coal in his hand... from the alter. With it, he touched my mouth and said, 'See, this has touched your lips; your guilt is taken away and your sin atoned for.'"*

Lesson: Isaiah saw God's holiness and realized his own sinfulness. But God cleansed him, preparing him for service.

Reflection: Do you acknowledge your need for God's cleansing, or do you try to serve Him while holding onto sin?

Challenge: Take time today to confess anything that is separating you from God. Ask Him to cleanse you and renew your heart.

Day 3: Trusting in God's Promises

Scripture: *Isaiah 40:31 – "But those who hope in the LORD will renew their strength. They will soar on wings like eagles; they will run and not grow weary, they will walk and not be faint."*

Lesson: Isaiah encouraged people to trust in God's strength, not their own. Waiting on God leads to renewal.

Reflection: Are you relying on your own strength to get through difficulties, or are you placing your hope in God?

Challenge: If you're feeling weary, take time today to rest in God's presence. Read Isaiah 40 and find peace in His promises.

Day 4: God's Ways Are Higher Than Ours

Scripture: *Isaiah 55:8-9 – "'For my thoughts are not your thoughts, neither are your ways my ways,' declares the Lord. 'As the heavens are higher than the earth, so are my ways higher than your ways and my thoughts than your thoughts.'"*

Lesson: Isaiah reminded Israel that God's plans are greater than human understanding. We must trust Him, even when life doesn't make sense.

Reflection: Do you struggle with wanting to understand everything before trusting God? Are you willing to surrender your plans to Him?

Challenge: Write down a situation where you've been struggling to trust God. Pray and surrender it fully to Him today.

Day 5: The Promise of the Messiah

Scripture: *Isaiah 9:6 – "For to us a child is born, to us a son is given... And he will be called Wonderful Counselor, Mighty God, Everlasting Father, Prince of Peace."*

Lesson: Isaiah prophesied about Jesus centuries before His birth. God's promises are sure, and His salvation plan is perfect.

Reflection: Do you live with the confidence that Jesus is your Wonderful Counselor, Mighty God, and Prince of Peace? How does this change your daily life?

Challenge: Take a moment today to thank God for Jesus. Meditate on who He is and what His birth means for your life.

Final Summary: What Isaiah Teaches Us

- **Day 1:** Be willing to say "Yes" to God's call.
- **Day 2:** Acknowledge your need for cleansing and renewal.
- **Day 3:** Trust in God's strength, not your own.
- **Day 4:** Accept that God's ways are beyond our understanding.
- **Day 5:** Rejoice in the promise of Jesus, our Savior.

Life Application: Which lesson spoke to you the most? How will you live it out moving forward? Pray for the courage to trust God fully, serve Him faithfully, and rest in His promises.

Chapter 34

Jeremiah: A Life of Faithfulness in the Face of Opposition

(Jeremiah)

Day 1: Called Before Birth

Scripture: *Jeremiah 1:5 – "Before I formed you in the womb I knew you, before you were born I set you apart; I appointed you as a prophet to the nations."*

Lesson: Jeremiah didn't choose his calling—God had a plan for him before he was even born. He was set apart for a divine purpose.

Reflection: Do you believe that God has a unique plan for your life? Are you walking in that calling?

Challenge: Take time today to reflect on your gifts and how God may want to use them. Ask Him to reveal His purpose for your life.

Day 2: Overcoming Fear and Insecurity

Scripture: *Jeremiah 1:6-8 – "'Alas, Sovereign LORD,' I said, 'I do not know how to speak; I am too young.' But the LORD said to me, 'Do not say, "I am too young." You must go to everyone I send you to and say whatever I command you. Do not be afraid of them, for I am with you...'"*

Lesson: Jeremiah felt unqualified, but God reassured him that He would be with him. God doesn't call the qualified—He qualifies the called.

Reflection: Are you allowing fear or insecurity to hold you back from what God is calling you to do?

Challenge: Step out in faith today in an area where you feel unqualified. Trust that God will equip you as you obey.

Day 3: Faithfulness in a Rebellious World

Scripture: *Jeremiah 7:27 – "When you tell them all this, they will not listen to you; when you call to them, they will not answer."*

Lesson: God warned Jeremiah that people would reject his message, but he was still called to be faithful. Obedience to God matters more than results.

Reflection: Do you stay faithful to God even when it feels like no one is listening or appreciating your efforts?

Challenge: If you're facing discouragement, keep going. Encourage someone else today, even if you don't see immediate results.

Day 4: God's Word as a Fire in Our Hearts

Scripture: *Jeremiah 20:9 – "...His word is in my heart like a fire, a fire shut up in my bones. I am weary of holding it in; indeed, I cannot."*

Lesson: Jeremiah wanted to stop preaching because of opposition, but God's word burned within him—he couldn't stay silent.

Reflection: Do you have a passion for sharing God's truth, or have you allowed opposition or complacency to silence you?

Challenge: Share your faith today in some way—through a conversation, social media, or an act of love. Let God's word be a fire in you.

Day 5: Hope in God's Future Plans

Scripture: *Jeremiah 29:11 – "For I know the plans I have for you, declares the Lord, plans to prosper you and not to harm you, plans to give you hope and a future."*

Lesson: Even though Jeremiah preached to a rebellious nation, God's message remained one of hope—He had a plan for restoration.

Reflection: Are you trusting in God's good plans for your future, even when things seem difficult?

Challenge: Write down one area of your life where you need to trust God's plan. Surrender it to Him in prayer today.

Final Summary: What Jeremiah Teaches Us

- **Day 1:** God has a purpose for you—embrace it.
- **Day 2:** Don't let fear stop you—God equips the called.
- **Day 3:** Stay faithful, even when no one listens.
- **Day 4:** Let God's word burn in your heart—don't stay silent.
- **Day 5:** Trust in God's plan for your future.

Life Application: Which lesson inspired you the most? How will you incorporate it into your life moving forward? Pray for boldness, perseverance, and faith in God's calling for your life.

Chapter 35

Ezekiel: A Life of Vision, Obedience, and Restoration

(Ezekiel)

Day 1: Called to Speak, Even When It's Hard

Scripture: *Ezekiel 2:6-7 – "And you, son of man, do not be afraid of them or their words... You must speak my words to them, whether they listen or fail to listen, for they are rebellious."*

Lesson: God called Ezekiel to be His prophet to a stubborn people. He was commanded to speak truth, even if people rejected him.

Reflection: Are you hesitant to share God's truth because you fear rejection?

Challenge: Be bold today—share a biblical truth with someone, whether in a conversation, on social media, or through an encouraging message.

Day 2: Being Led by the Spirit

Scripture: *Ezekiel 3:12 – "Then the Spirit lifted me up, and I heard behind me a loud rumbling sound as the glory of the Lord rose from the place where it was standing."*

Lesson: Ezekiel's ministry was guided by the Holy Spirit. He didn't act on his own ideas but followed God's leading.

Reflection: Are you seeking God's direction in your life, or are you making decisions based on your own wisdom?

Challenge: Pray today for the Holy Spirit's guidance in a decision you need to make. Be still and listen for His direction.

Day 3: Taking Responsibility for Others

Scripture: *Ezekiel 3:18 – "When I say to a wicked person, 'You will surely die,' and you do not warn them or speak out to dissuade them from their evil ways... I will hold you accountable for their blood."*

Lesson: Ezekiel was called to warn others. If he stayed silent, he would be held responsible for their destruction.

Reflection: Are you willing to lovingly warn people about sin and encourage them toward God?

Challenge: Reach out to someone today who may be struggling spiritually. Encourage them with God's truth and love.

Day 4: Trusting in God's Power Over Dry Bones

Scripture: *Ezekiel 37:3 – "He asked me, 'Son of man, can these bones live?' I said, 'Sovereign LORD, you alone know.'"*

Lesson: Ezekiel saw a vision of dry bones coming back to life, symbolizing Israel's restoration. No situation is too dead for God to revive.

Reflection: Are there areas in your life that feel hopeless? Do you believe God can restore what seems lost?

Challenge: Pray over a "dry bones" situation in your life today—something that seems beyond fixing. Trust God to bring restoration in His way and time.

Day 5: God's Presence Restored

Scripture: *Ezekiel 48:35 – "...And the name of the city from that time on will be: THE LORD IS THERE."*

Lesson: Ezekiel's final vision was of God's presence fully restored. No matter what we go through, God's ultimate plan is to dwell with His people.

Reflection: Are you living in a way that welcomes God's presence daily?

Challenge: Take time today to intentionally dwell in God's presence—through worship, prayer, or reading His Word without distraction.

Final Summary: What Ezekiel Teaches Us

- **Day 1:** Speak God's truth, even when it's hard.
- **Day 2:** Be led by the Holy Spirit, not your own wisdom.
- **Day 3:** Take responsibility for encouraging others spiritually.
- **Day 4:** Trust God to bring life where there seems to be none.
- **Day 5:** Seek and dwell in God's presence daily.

Life Application: Which lesson struck you the most? How will you let it affect your decisions moving forward? Ask God for boldness, trust, and a deeper awareness of His presence in your life.

Chapter 36

Daniel: A Life of Unshakable Faith, Prayer, and Godly Influence

(Daniel)

Day 1: Purposeful Living and Uncompromising Conviction

Scripture: *Daniel 1:8 – "But Daniel resolved not to defile himself with the royal food and wine, and he asked the chief official for permission not to defile himself this way."*

Lesson: Daniel made a decision early on to honor God, refusing to compromise his values, even in a foreign land. His resolve shaped his destiny and influenced his peers.

Reflection: Are you living with purpose and conviction, or are you compromising to fit in?

Challenge: Identify one area where you've been tempted to compromise. Resolve today to stand firm in your faith and values, regardless of pressure.

Day 2: Prayer as a Non-Negotiable Priority

Scripture: *Daniel 6:10 – "Now when Daniel learned that the decree had been published, he went home to his upstairs room where the windows opened toward Jerusalem. Three times a day he got down on his knees and prayed, giving thanks to his God, just as he had done before."*

Lesson: Daniel's prayer life was consistent and unwavering, even when it became illegal. His discipline in prayer was the secret to his strength and courage.

Reflection: Is prayer a non-negotiable priority in your life, or is it something you only do when convenient?

Challenge: Commit to a consistent prayer routine today. Spend intentional time in prayer, no matter how busy or challenging your day is.

Day 3: Trusting God in the Face of Danger

Scripture: *Daniel 6:16 – "Daniel answered, '…My God sent his angel, and he shut the mouths of the lions. They have not hurt me, because I was found innocent in his sight…'…And when Daniel was lifted from the den, no wound was found on him, because he had trusted in his God."*

Lesson: Daniel trusted God even when thrown into the lions' den. His faith wasn't dependent on his circumstances but on his unshakeable confidence in God's power and goodness.

Reflection: Do you trust God even when faced with danger, uncertainty, or persecution?

Challenge: Identify one fear or challenge you're facing. Surrender it to God today, trusting Him completely regardless of the outcome.

Day 4: Humility and Wisdom in Leadership

Scripture: *Daniel 2:27-28 – "Daniel replied, 'No wise man, enchanter, magician or diviner can explain to the king the mystery he has asked about, but there is a God in heaven who reveals mysteries…'"*

Lesson: Daniel gave all the glory to God when interpreting King Nebuchadnezzar's dream. His humility and wisdom set him apart as a leader in a foreign land.

Reflection: Are you giving God the credit for your successes and abilities, or are you taking glory for yourself?

Challenge: Acknowledge God's hand in your achievements today. Give Him the glory in your conversations and actions.

Day 5: Perseverance in Seeking Understanding and Revelation

Scripture: *Daniel 10:12 – "Then he continued, 'Do not be afraid, Daniel. Since the first day that you set your mind to gain understanding and to humble yourself before your God, your words were heard, and I have come in response to them.'"*

Lesson: Daniel persisted in prayer and fasting for 21 days to seek understanding of a vision. His perseverance brought divine revelation and insight.

Reflection: Are you persevering in prayer and seeking God's wisdom, or do you give up easily?

Challenge: Pray and seek God today for wisdom or understanding in a situation. Commit to persevering in prayer until you receive clarity.

Final Summary: What Daniel Teaches Us

- **Day 1:** Live with purpose—don't compromise your values.
- **Day 2:** Make prayer a priority—stay consistent in seeking God.
- **Day 3:** Trust God in adversity—have unshakeable faith in His power.
- **Day 4:** Lead with humility—give God the glory in all things.
- **Day 5:** Persevere in prayer—seek understanding and revelation from God.

Life Application: Which lesson challenged you the most? How will you continue to apply it in your life? Pray for a heart like Daniel's—steadfast in faith, committed in prayer, and courageous in conviction.

CHAPTER 37

SHADRACH, MESHACH, AND ABEDNEGO: UNWAVERING FAITH, COURAGE, AND GOD'S DELIVERANCE

(DANIEL 1-3)

Day 1: Standing Firm in Conviction

Scripture: *Daniel 3:12 – "But there are some Jews whom you have set over the affairs of the province of Babylon—Shadrach, Meshach, and Abednego—who pay no attention to you, Your Majesty. They neither serve your gods nor worship the image of gold you have set up."*

Lesson: Shadrach, Meshach, and Abednego refused to compromise their faith, even when faced with the pressure to conform. They stood firm in their convictions, knowing that God's approval mattered more than man's.

Reflection: Are you standing firm in your faith, or are you compromising to fit in or avoid conflict?

Challenge: Identify one area where you've been tempted to compromise. Commit to standing firm in your faith today, regardless of peer pressure or opposition.

Day 2: Courage to Face Consequences

Scripture: *Daniel 3:16-18 – "Shadrach, Meshach, and Abednego replied to him, 'King Nebuchadnezzar, we do not need to defend ourselves before you in this matter. If we are* *thrown into the blazing furnace, the God we serve is able to deliver us from it... But even if He does not, we want you to know, Your Majesty, that we will not serve your gods or worship the image of gold you have set up.'"*

Lesson: Their faith was not based on the outcome but on God's character. They believed God could save them but were prepared to face the consequences if He chose not to.

Reflection: Is your faith dependent on getting the outcome you want, or do you trust God regardless of the result?

Challenge: Surrender a situation to God today, trusting Him with the outcome. Declare, "Even if it doesn't go my way, I will still trust and serve You, Lord."

Day 3: The Presence of God in the Fire

Scripture: *Daniel 3:24-25 – "Then King Nebuchadnezzar leaped to his feet in amazement and asked his advisers, 'Weren't there three men that we tied up and threw into the fire?' They replied, 'Certainly, Your Majesty.' He said, 'Look! I see four men walking around in the fire, unbound and unharmed, and the fourth looks like a son of the gods.'"*

Lesson: God didn't prevent them from entering the fire, but He joined them in it. His presence protected them, showing that we are never alone in our trials.

Reflection: Do you trust that God is with you in your struggles, or do you feel abandoned in difficult times?

Challenge: Acknowledge God's presence in your current challenges. Speak His promises over your life: "I am not alone. God is with me in this fire."

Day 4: Deliverance Without a Trace of Harm

Scripture: *Daniel 3:27 – "...They saw that the fire had not harmed their bodies, nor was a hair of their heads singed; their robes were not scorched, and there was no smell of fire on them."*

Lesson: God delivered Shadrach, Meshach, and Abednego completely—without even the smell of smoke. He not only protects but also restores beyond expectation.

Reflection: Do you believe that God can not only bring you through trials but also restore and redeem every part of your life?

Challenge: Pray for complete restoration today in any area where you've faced difficulty. Trust God to bring you through and heal even lingering harm.

Day 5: Impacting Others Through Faith

Scripture: *Daniel 3:28-29 – "Then Nebuchadnezzar said, 'Praise be to the God of Shadrach, Meshach, and Abednego... Therefore I decree that the people of any nation or language who say anything against the God of Shadrach, Meshach, and Abednego be cut into pieces and their houses be turned into piles of rubble, for no other god can save in this way.'"*

Lesson: Their faith influenced a pagan king and led to a public declaration of God's power. When we stand firm, others see God's glory through our testimony.

Reflection: Are you living in a way that reflects God's power and impacts others?

Challenge: Share your testimony today—how God has delivered or sustained you. Let your faith inspire someone else.

Final Summary: What Shadrach, Meshach, and Abednego Teach Us

- **Day 1:** Stand firm in your faith—don't compromise your convictions.
- **Day 2:** Trust God regardless of the outcome—faith isn't conditional.
- **Day 3:** Remember God's presence—He is with you in the fire.
- **Day 4:** Believe in complete deliverance—God restores and redeems.
- **Day 5:** Let your faith impact others—your testimony brings God glory.

Life Application: Which lesson spoke to you the most? How will you continue to carry it out? Pray for faith like Shadrach, Meshach, and Abednego—unwavering, courageous, and trusting in God's power and presence.

Chapter 38

Nehemiah: A Life of Leadership, Prayer, and Perseverance

(Nehemiah)

Day 1: Having a Heart for God's Work

Scripture: *Nehemiah 1:4 – "When I heard these things, I sat down and wept. For some days I mourned and fasted and prayed before the God of heaven."*

Lesson: Nehemiah was deeply moved when he heard about the broken state of Jerusalem. His first response wasn't action—it was prayer.

Reflection: Do you have a heart for God's work? Do you take your burdens to Him in prayer first, or do you rush into action?

Challenge: Take time today to pray for something that breaks your heart. Ask God how He wants you to be involved in His work.

Day 2: Boldness to Act

Scripture: *Nehemiah 2:4-5 – "The king said to me, 'What is it you want?' Then I prayed to the God of heaven, and I answered the king,... send me to the city in Judah where my ancestors are buried so that I can rebuild it.'"*

Lesson: Nehemiah had the courage to ask a foreign, occupying king for resources to rebuild Jerusalem. He prayed in the moment, then boldly stepped forward in faith.

Reflection: Are you willing to step out in faith when God opens doors? Do you hesitate because of fear or uncertainty?

Challenge: Take one bold step today toward something you know God is calling you to do. Pray, then act.

Day 3: Overcoming Opposition

Scripture: *Nehemiah 4:14 – "...Don't be afraid of them. Remember the Lord, who is great and awesome, and fight for your families, your sons and your daughters, your wives and your homes."*

Lesson: Nehemiah faced constant opposition from enemies who wanted to stop the rebuilding of Jerusalem. He reminded the people to focus on God and keep fighting.

Reflection: Do you get discouraged when facing opposition? Are you relying on your own strength or on God?

Challenge: Identify a challenge in your life and choose to fight through it with God's help. Declare His power over your situation.

Day 4: Staying Focused on the Mission

Scripture: *Nehemiah 6:3 – "...'I am carrying on a great project and cannot go down. Why should the work stop while I leave it and go down to you?'"*

Lesson: When Nehemiah's enemies tried to distract him, he refused to be pulled away from the work God had given him.

Reflection: Are distractions keeping you from what God has called you to do?

Challenge: Identify one distraction in your life and take a step to remove or minimize it so you can focus on your purpose in the Lord.

Day 5: Leading by Example

Scripture: *Nehemiah 5:16 – "Instead, I devoted myself to the work on this wall. All my men were assembled there for the work; we did not acquire any land."*

Lesson: Nehemiah didn't just tell people what to do—he led by example. He worked alongside the people, showing integrity and commitment.

Reflection: Are you leading by example in your family, workplace, and community?

Challenge: Lead by example today in one specific area—whether in your work ethic, faithfulness, or generosity.

Final Summary: What Nehemiah Teaches Us

- **Day 1:** Have a heart for God's work—pray before acting.
- **Day 2:** Be bold—step out in faith when God opens doors.
- **Day 3:** Persevere through opposition—God fights for you.
- **Day 4:** Stay focused—don't let distractions pull you away from your mission.
- **Day 5:** Lead by example—your actions inspire others.

Life Application: Which lesson do you need to practice the most? How will you incorporate it going forward? Pray for strength to live with boldness, perseverance, and focus as you pursue what God has called you to do.

Chapter 39

Ezra: A Life of Devotion, Obedience, and Revival

(Ezra)

Day 1: Preparing Your Heart for God's Word

Scripture: *Ezra 7:10 – "For Ezra had devoted himself to the study and observance of the Law of the Lord, and to teaching its decrees and laws in Israel."*

Lesson: Ezra didn't just study God's Word—he lived it and taught it. This devotion was the foundation of his leadership and revival work.

Reflection: Are you actively studying and applying God's Word in your daily life?

Challenge: Spend extra time in the Bible today. Choose a passage, meditate on it, and find a way to apply it.

Day 2: Courage to Restore What Is Broken

Scripture: *Ezra 1:3 – "While Ezra was praying and confessing, weeping and throwing himself down before the house of God, a large crowd of Israelites—men, women and children—gathered around him. They too wept bitterly."*

Lesson: Ezra not only led the effort to rebuild the temple and restore worship in Jerusalem, but also led the way in repentance for the sins of his people and restoration of righteousness. He stepped up to restore what had been broken both physically and spiritually.

Reflection: Is there something in your life—spiritually or relationally—that needs restoration?

Challenge: Take one step today toward rebuilding something broken, whether it's a relationship, habit, or area of faith.

Day 3: Trusting God Through Challenges

Scripture: *Ezra 8:21 – "There, by the Ahava Canal, I proclaimed a fast, so that we might humble ourselves before our God and ask Him for a safe journey..."*

Lesson: Ezra and his people traveled without a military escort, relying completely on God's protection. Their faith led them to fast and pray instead of seeking human help.

Reflection: Are you trusting in God's provision and protection, or do you rely only on your own strength?

Challenge: Fast from something today (a meal, social media, etc.) and spend that time in prayer, asking God for guidance in a specific area.

Day 4: Confronting Sin with a Heart of Repentance

Scripture: *Ezra 9:6 – "...I am too ashamed and disgraced, my God, to lift up my face to you, because our sins are higher than our heads and our guilt has reached to the heavens."*

Lesson: Ezra grieved over Israel's sins and led them in repentance. He understood that revival begins with a humble heart.

Reflection: Are there areas in your life where sin has gone unchecked? Have you brought them before God in repentance?

Challenge: Spend time today examining your heart. Confess anything that separates you from God and ask for His cleansing and renewal. If there is sin in your family, lead by example and lead your family in a corporate prayer of repentance.

Day 5: Leading Others to Spiritual Renewal

Scripture: *Ezra 10:11 – "Now honor the Lord, the God of your ancestors, and do His will. Separate yourselves from the peoples around you and from your foreign wives."*

Lesson: Ezra called the people to make radical changes to obey God fully. True spiritual renewal requires action, not just emotion.

Reflection: Are you willing to make necessary changes to follow God more closely?

Challenge: Make a concrete decision today to remove anything that is pulling you away from God—whether a habit, relationship, entertainment, or distraction.

Final Summary: What Ezra Teaches Us

- **Day 1:** Study and apply God's Word—it is the foundation of spiritual life.
- **Day 2:** Be courageous in restoring what is broken.
- **Day 3:** Trust God's protection and provision—seek Him first.
- **Day 4:** Confront sin and lead with repentance.
- **Day 5:** Spiritual renewal requires action—commit to full obedience.

Life Application: Which lesson stood out to you the most? How will you practice it moving forward? Pray for strength to pursue spiritual renewal, obedience, and leadership in your own life.

MAKE A DIFFERENCE WITH YOUR REVIEW

Encourage Someone on Their Faith Journey

"As iron sharpens iron, so one person sharpens another." – Proverbs 27:17

Spiritual growth is not meant to be a solo journey. Just as we learn from the lives of the men in this devotional, we can also **help and encourage others** by sharing what God is teaching us.

Would you take a moment to help someone—just like you—who is looking for a way to grow closer to God but isn't sure where to start?

My mission with **The Ultimate Devotional for Busy Men** is to make **spiritual reflection simple, practical, and meaningful**, even in the busiest of seasons. But to reach more men who need this encouragement, I need your help.

Most people choose books based on reviews. Your **honest review** could make all the difference for a man searching for a devotional that fits his life.

It costs nothing and takes less than a minute, but your review could help...

- **One more husband become a stronger spiritual leader in his home.**
- **One more father raise his children with wisdom and faith.**
- **One more man find strength in God during a tough season.**
- **One more believer stay grounded in truth during daily challenges.**

To leave a review, simply scan the QR code below or visit:

[https://www.amazon.com/review/review-your-purchases/?asin=B0F4P1S3YV]

If this devotional has encouraged you, would you pay it forward? **Your words could be the reason another man finds the encouragement he needs.**

Thank you for taking this journey with me. May God continue to strengthen you as you grow in faith!

- **David Powell**

Chapter 40

Jonah: A Life of Obedience, Mercy, and God's Sovereignty

(Jonah)

Day 1: Running from God's Call

Scripture: *Jonah 1:3 – "But Jonah ran away from the LORD and headed for Tarshish..."*

Lesson: Jonah resisted God's call because he didn't want to obey. He ran in the opposite direction, thinking he could escape God's plan.

Reflection: Are you avoiding something that God is calling you to do? Are you letting fear, pride, or reluctance keep you from obedience?

Challenge: Identify one area where you've been hesitant to obey God. Take a step today in the direction of obedience.

Day 2: God's Discipline Leads to Repentance

Scripture: *Jonah 2:1 – "From inside the fish Jonah prayed to the LORD his God."*

Lesson: God used a storm and a great fish to redirect Jonah. Sometimes, God allows difficulties to bring us back to Him.

Reflection: Has God used challenges in your life to get your attention? Have you responded with repentance?

Challenge: If you're facing a trial, ask God what He wants to teach you. Spend time in prayer, acknowledging His sovereignty over your life.

Day 3: Obeying Even When It's Hard

Scripture: *Jonah 3:3 – "Jonah obeyed the word of the LORD and went to Nineveh..."*

Lesson: After his time in the fish, Jonah obeyed God and preached in Nineveh. Obedience, even when delayed, is always better than continued rebellion.

Reflection: Is there something God has asked you to do that you've been putting off? How can you take action today?

Challenge: Take a step of obedience today, no matter how small. Trust that God's plan is greater than your fears.

Day 4: God's Mercy is for Everyone

Scripture: *Jonah 3:10 – "When God saw what they did and how they turned from their evil ways, He relented and did not bring on them the destruction He had threatened."*

Lesson: Jonah was upset when God showed mercy to Nineveh. He wanted justice, but God desires repentance and redemption.

Reflection: Do you struggle to extend mercy to those you think don't deserve it? Are you willing to love as God loves?

Challenge: Forgive someone today who has wronged you. Extend the same mercy to others that God has given you.

Day 5: Letting Go of Selfishness and Bitterness

Scripture: *Jonah 4:11 – "And should I not have concern for the great city of Nineveh, in which there are more than a hundred and twenty thousand people...?"*

Lesson: Jonah cared more about his own comfort than the salvation of others. He was bitter instead of rejoicing in God's grace.

Reflection: Are you holding onto bitterness or selfishness instead of aligning your heart with God's?

Challenge: Ask God to help you see others as He does. Let go of any bitterness, resentment, or selfish desires, and choose to rejoice in God's grace.

Final Summary: What Jonah Teaches Us

- **Day 1:** Stop running from God's call—embrace obedience.
- **Day 2:** God's discipline is for our growth—learn from challenges.
- **Day 3:** Obedience brings blessing—step out in faith.
- **Day 4:** God's mercy extends to everyone—practice forgiveness.
- **Day 5:** Align your heart with God's—let go of bitterness.

Life Application: Which lesson convicted you the most? How will you let it affect you moving forward? Pray for a heart that obeys, forgives, and rejoices in God's mercy for all people.

Chapter 41

Hosea: Unfailing Love, Faithfulness, and God's Redemption

(Hosea)

Day 1: A Calling to Demonstrate God's Love

Scripture: *Hosea 1:2 – "When the LORD began to speak through Hosea, the LORD said to him, 'Go, marry a promiscuous woman and have children with her, for like an adulterous wife this land is guilty of unfaithfulness to the LORD.'"*

Lesson: Hosea was called to live out a real-life picture of God's love for Israel. His marriage to an unfaithful wife symbolized God's love for His people, even when they turned away from Him.

Reflection: Are you showing God's love even when it is difficult or undeserved?

Challenge: Choose one person today to love unconditionally, even if they have disappointed or hurt you.

Day 2: Love That Pursues and Redeems

Scripture: *Hosea 3:1 – "The LORD said to me, 'Go, show your love to your wife again, though she is loved by another man and is an adulteress. Love her as the LORD loves the Israelites, though they turn to other gods...'"*

Lesson: Hosea pursued and redeemed his unfaithful wife, just as God continues to pursue us despite our failures. His love is relentless and seeks to restore us.

Reflection: Have you ever resisted God's love and grace, yet He still pursued you?

Challenge: Take time today to reflect on God's relentless love for you, and extend that same grace to someone in need of forgiveness in your life.

Day 3: The Pain of Unfaithfulness

Scripture: *Hosea 4:1 – "Hear the word of the LORD, you Israelites, because the LORD has a charge to bring against you who live in the land: 'There is no faithfulness, no love, no acknowledgment of God in the land.'"*

Lesson: God's heart was broken over Israel's unfaithfulness, just as a spouse is deeply hurt by betrayal. Our sin isn't just about breaking rules—it's about breaking God's heart.

Reflection: Are there areas in your life where you've been unfaithful to God, placing other things before Him?

Challenge: Identify one "idol" in your life that is pulling your focus away from God. Confess it and take steps to put God first again—to love Him above all else.

Day 4: God's Discipline and Call to Return

Scripture: *Hosea 6:1 – "Come, let us return to the LORD. He has torn us to pieces but He will heal us; He has injured us but He will bind up our wounds."*

Lesson: Though God disciplines His people, His purpose is always to heal and restore them. His correction is motivated by love, not anger.

Reflection: Are you resisting God's discipline, or are you allowing it to lead you back to Him?

Challenge: If you are going through a season of correction, embrace it as an opportunity for growth. Ask God to use it to deepen your relationship with Him.

Day 5: God's Unbreakable Love and Mercy

Scripture: *Hosea 11:8-9 – "How can I give you up, Ephraim? How can I hand you over, Israel?... My heart is changed within Me; all My compassion is aroused. I will not carry out My fierce anger, nor will I devastate Ephraim again. For I am God, and not a man—the Holy One among you..."*

Lesson: Even after Israel's repeated rebellion, God's love remains steadfast. He did not give up on His people, just as He never gives up on us.

Reflection: Do you fully trust in God's mercy, or do you struggle with guilt and shame?

Challenge: Accept God's forgiveness fully today. Release any lingering guilt and walk in the freedom of His unfailing love.

Final Summary: What Hosea Teaches Us

- **Day 1:** Love even when it's hard—God loves us despite our failures.
- **Day 2:** God pursues and redeems—His love never gives up.
- **Day 3:** Sin breaks God's heart—stay faithful in your relationship with Him.
- **Day 4:** God's discipline leads to healing—trust Him in times of correction.
- **Day 5:** God's love is unbreakable—His mercy is greater than our failures.

Life Application: Which lesson challenged you the most? How will you let it affect your decisions moving forward? Pray for a heart like Hosea's—one that reflects God's love, pursues others with grace, and remains faithful no matter the circumstances.

Chapter 42

Malachi: A Life of Faithfulness, Honor, and True Worship

(Malachi)

Day 1: Giving God Your Best

Scripture: *Malachi 1:8 – "When you offer blind animals for sacrifice, is that not wrong? When you sacrifice lame or diseased animals, is that not wrong? Try offering them to your governor! Would he be pleased with you?..."*

Lesson: The people in Malachi's time gave God their leftovers instead of their best. God desires our wholehearted devotion, not just empty rituals.

Reflection: Are you giving God your best in your time, talents, and worship, or are you offering Him what's leftover?

Challenge: Examine how you spend your time and energy. Make a commitment today to give God your best, whether in prayer, worship, time, or service.

Day 2: Honoring God in Our Relationships

Scripture: *Malachi 2:16 – "'The man who hates and divorces his wife,' says the LORD, the God of Israel, 'does violence to the one he should protect...'"*

Lesson: Malachi rebuked the people for breaking their commitments, especially in marriage. God values faithfulness in all relationships.

Reflection: Are you honoring God in your relationships—with your spouse, family, friends, or coworkers?

Challenge: Strengthen one relationship today by being intentional—ask for forgiveness where needed and offer forgiveness, encouragement, or a loving act of service.

Day 3: Returning to God with a Sincere Heart

Scripture: *Malachi 3:7 – "...Return to me, and I will return to you, says the Lord Almighty..."*

Lesson: God invited His people to return to Him, but they didn't realize they had drifted away. He is always ready to restore us when we seek Him sincerely.

Reflection: Are there areas of your life where you've drifted from God without realizing it?

Challenge: Spend time in prayer today asking God to reveal any areas where you need to return to Him.

Day 4: Trusting God with Our Resources

Scripture: *Malachi 3:10 – "Bring the whole tithe into the storehouse, that there may be food in my house. Test me in this, says the LORD Almighty, and see if I will not throw open the floodgates of heaven and pour out so much blessing that there will not be room enough to store it."*

Lesson: God challenged His people to trust Him with their resources. When we put Him first, He provides abundantly.

Reflection: Are you trusting God with your finances and resources, or are you holding back?

Challenge: Give generously today—whether through tithing, helping someone in need, or using your time and talents to serve others.

Day 5: Living in Expectation of Christ's Return

Scripture: *Malachi 4:2 – "But for you who revere my name, the sun of righteousness will rise with healing in its rays..."*

Lesson: Malachi ends with a prophecy about the coming of Christ. Just as they waited for the Messiah's first coming, we now wait for His return.

Reflection: Are you living with a sense of expectation, preparing your heart for Christ's return?

Challenge: Live today with eternity in mind—share your faith, love others, and stay committed to walking in righteousness.

Final Summary: What Malachi Teaches Us

- **Day 1:** Give God your best—He deserves wholehearted devotion.
- **Day 2:** Honor God in your relationships—be faithful and loving.
- **Day 3:** Return to God with sincerity—He welcomes you back.
- **Day 4:** Trust God with your resources—He provides for those who give.
- **Day 5:** Live in expectation—Christ is coming again.

Life Application: Which lesson resonated with you most? How will you continue to apply it in your life? Pray for a heart that worships God fully, lives with integrity, and trusts Him completely.

Chapter 43

John the Baptist: A Life of Purpose, Humility, and Boldness

(Matthew 3,11,14; Mark 1,6; Luke 1,3,7; John 1,3)

Day 1: Called to Prepare the Way

Scripture: *Luke 3:4 – "...A voice of one calling in the wilderness, 'Prepare the way for the Lord, make straight paths for him.'"*

Lesson: John the Baptist's mission was clear—he was called to prepare people's hearts for Jesus. He lived with purpose and urgency.

Reflection: Are you living with a sense of purpose, preparing yourself and others for Christ?

Challenge: Ask God today how He wants to use you to prepare others for Jesus. Look for an opportunity to share your faith or encourage someone spiritually.

Day 2: A Life of Humility

Scripture: *John 3:30 – "He must become greater; I must become less."*

Lesson: John knew that his role was not to seek fame but to point people to Jesus. He willingly stepped aside when Christ began His ministry.

Reflection: Are you seeking recognition for yourself, or are you pointing others to Christ?

Challenge: Choose humility today. Instead of seeking personal credit, look for ways to honor God and lift others up.

Day 3: Boldly Speaking the Truth

Scripture: *Matthew 3:7-8 – "But when he saw many of the Pharisees and Sadducees coming to where he was baptizing, he said to them: 'You brood of vipers! Who warned you to flee from the coming wrath? Produce fruit in keeping with repentance.'"*

Lesson: John spoke the truth fearlessly, even to powerful leaders. His courage led people to repentance but also brought him persecution.

Reflection: Are you bold in sharing the truth of God's Word, even when it's uncomfortable?

Challenge: Speak the truth in love today. If you've been avoiding a tough conversation about faith, ask God for courage and wisdom to address it and take a step forward.

Day 4: Living a Simple and Focused Life

Scripture: *Matthew 3:4 – "John's clothes were made of camel's hair, and he had a leather belt around his waist. His food was locusts and wild honey."*

Lesson: John didn't seek wealth or comfort. He focused on his mission and lived simply, showing that a meaningful life isn't about material things.

Reflection: Are distractions, materialism, or worldly concerns keeping you from fully focusing on God?

Challenge: Simplify something in your life today. Whether it's decluttering, fasting from unnecessary distractions, or prioritizing time with God, choose to focus on what truly matters.

Day 5: Finishing Strong Despite Hardships

Scripture: *Matthew 11:6 – "Blessed is anyone who does not stumble on account of me."*

Lesson: John began to question if Jesus was the Messiah while he was sitting in prison, not experiencing the miracles he was hearing about. Jesus warned John not to be offended when circumstances did not meet his expectations.

Reflection: Are there any areas of your life where you have been offended at God for how He handled a situation?

Challenge: Examine your heart, if you are holding any offense toward God from your past or your present circumstances, bring that to the Lord honestly and repent for holding onto that offense or bitterness. Confess again your trust in the Lord's goodness and sovereignty, even when you don't understand.

Final Summary: What John the Baptist Teaches Us

- **Day 1:** Live with purpose—prepare the way for Christ.
- **Day 2:** Choose humility—point others to Jesus, not yourself.
- **Day 3:** Be bold—speak the truth with courage.
- **Day 4:** Focus on what matters—don't let material things distract you.
- **Day 5:** Stay faithful—don't be offended when things are different than you expected.

Life Application: Which lesson spoke to you most? How will you carry it out moving forward? Pray for a heart like John's—bold, humble, and fully committed to God's mission.

Chapter 44

Jesus Christ: The Perfect Example of Love, Humility, and Obedience

(Matthew; Mark; Luke; John)

Day 1: A Life of Humility and Servanthood

Scripture: *Philippians 2:5-7 – "In your relationships with one another, have the same mindset as Christ Jesus: Who, being in very nature God, did not consider equality with God something to be used to His own advantage; rather, he made himself nothing by taking the very nature of a servant..."*

Lesson: Jesus, though fully God, chose to humble Himself and serve others. He washed His disciples' feet and lived a life of sacrifice.

Reflection: Are you willing to humble yourself and serve others as Jesus did?

Challenge: Find one way to serve someone today, whether through an act of kindness, encouragement, or meeting a need without seeking recognition.

Day 2: Loving Even the Unlovable

Scripture: *Luke 6:35 – "But love your enemies, do good to them, and lend to them without expecting to get anything back. Then your reward will be great, and you will be children of the Most High..."*

Lesson: Jesus loved and forgave even those who betrayed, denied, and crucified Him. He calls us to love beyond our comfort.

Reflection: Is there someone in your life you find difficult to love or forgive?

Challenge: Pray for someone who has hurt you. Choose to extend grace and love, just as Jesus did.

Day 3: A Life of Prayer and Dependence on God

Scripture: *Mark 1:35 – "Very early in the morning, while it was still dark, Jesus got up, left the house and went off to a solitary place, where He prayed."*

Lesson: Even though Jesus was the Son of God, He constantly sought the Father in prayer. His strength and wisdom came from time alone with God.

Reflection: Are you prioritizing time with God daily, or do distractions get in the way?

Challenge: Set aside uninterrupted time today for prayer, no matter how busy you are. Seek God's presence like Jesus did.

Day 4: Obedience Even in Suffering

Scripture: *Luke 22:42 – "Father, if you are willing, take this cup from me; yet not my will, but yours be done."*

Lesson: Jesus willingly submitted to God's will, even when it meant suffering. He trusted God's plan above His own desires.

Reflection: Is there an area where you are struggling to obey God? Are you willing to trust His plan even when it's hard?

Challenge: Surrender one area of your life to God today. Pray, "Not my will, but Yours be done," and trust His perfect plan.

Day 5: The Power of the Resurrection

Scripture: *John 11:25 – "Jesus said to her, 'I am the resurrection and the life. The one who believes in me will live, even though they die.'"*

Lesson: Jesus' resurrection proves that He has power over sin and death. Because of Him, we have eternal life and victory over our struggles.

Reflection: Are you living with the confidence that Jesus has conquered sin, death, and every struggle you face?

Challenge: Walk in victory today! Declare the power of Jesus' resurrection over any fear, sin, or challenge in your life.

Final Summary: What Jesus Teaches Us

- **Day 1:** Serve with humility—true greatness is found in serving others.
- **Day 2:** Love your enemies—Jesus loved even those who betrayed Him.
- **Day 3:** Stay connected to God—prayer is your source of strength.
- **Day 4:** Obey even when it's hard—God's plan is always greater.
- **Day 5:** Walk in victory—Jesus has conquered sin and death!

Life Application: Which lesson inspired you the most? How will you practice it moving forward? Ask God to shape you into Christ's likeness—loving, obedient, and fully surrendered to His will.

Chapter 45

Peter: A Life of Boldness, Failure, and Redemption

(Matthew 4,8,10,14-19,26; Mark 1,3,5,8-9,13-14,16; Luke 4-6,8-9,12,22,24; John 1,6,13,18,20-21; Acts 1-12,15; I and II Peter)

Day 1: Called to Step Out in Faith

Scripture: *Matthew 14:29 – "'Come,' He said. Then Peter got down out of the boat, walked on the water and came toward Jesus."*

Lesson: Peter was the only disciple who had the faith to step out of the boat and walk on water. His willingness to trust Jesus led to a miraculous moment.

Reflection: Are you willing to take bold steps of faith, even when it seems impossible?

Challenge: Identify one area where fear has been holding you back. Take a step of faith today, trusting Jesus completely.

Day 2: When Faith Falters, Jesus Lifts Us Up

Scripture: *Matthew 14:30-31 – "But when he saw the wind, he was afraid and, beginning to sink, cried out, 'Lord, save me!' Immediately Jesus reached out His hand and caught him..."*

Lesson: Peter's faith wavered when he focused on the storm instead of Jesus. But even in doubt, Jesus immediately rescued him.

Reflection: Are you focusing on the storms in your life, or are you keeping your eyes on Jesus?

Challenge: If you feel overwhelmed, shift your focus back to Jesus today. Spend time in prayer and trust Him with your struggles.

Day 3: Learning from Failure

Scripture: *Luke 22:61-62 – "The Lord turned and looked straight at Peter. Then Peter remembered the word the Lord had spoken to him: 'Before the rooster crows today, you will disown me three times.' And he went outside and wept bitterly."*

Lesson: Peter denied Jesus three times, despite his earlier boldness and promises of loyalty. Yet his failure was not the end of his story—God still had a plan for him.

Reflection: Have you ever felt like you failed God? Do you believe He can still use you?

Challenge: If you're struggling with past mistakes, confess them to God today and fully accept God's forgiveness. Remember that failure is not final with Jesus.

Day 4: Restored and Given a New Purpose

Scripture: *John 21:17 – "The third time He said to him, 'Simon son of John, do you love me?' Peter was hurt because Jesus asked him the third time, 'Do you love me?' He said, 'Lord, you know all things; you know that I love you.' Jesus said, 'Feed my sheep.'"*

Lesson: Jesus restored Peter after his denial, giving him a new purpose—to shepherd His people. God turns failures into callings.

Reflection: Do you believe that Jesus can restore and use you, no matter what you've done?

Challenge: Ask God how He wants to use you in this season of your life. Be open to His calling.

Day 5: Boldly Proclaiming the Gospel

Scripture: *Acts 2:38 – "Peter replied, 'Repent and be baptized, every one of you, in the name of Jesus Christ for the forgiveness of your sins...'"*

Lesson: The same Peter who denied Jesus later preached boldly at Pentecost, leading thousands to Christ. A life surrendered to God has limitless impact.

Reflection: Are you willing to boldly share your faith, despite past mistakes or fears?

Challenge: Look for an opportunity today to share your faith, whether through a conversation, encouragement, or an act of kindness.

Final Summary: What Peter Teaches Us

- **Day 1:** Step out in faith—Jesus is calling you beyond your comfort zone.
- **Day 2:** Keep your eyes on Jesus—don't let fear sink your faith.
- **Day 3:** Learn from failure—God's grace is greater than your mistakes.
- **Day 4:** Let Jesus restore and use you—your past does not define you.
- **Day 5:** Share your faith boldly—a transformed life can impact many.

Life Application: Which lesson stood out to you the most? How will you incorporate it in your life going forward? Pray for boldness, faith, and the confidence to trust God's plan for your life, just like Peter.

Chapter 46

John (The Apostle): Love, Truth, and Deep Relationship with Jesus

(Matthew 4,10,17,26; Mark 1,3,5,9-10,14; Luke 5-6,8-9,22,24; John 13,18-21; Acts 1-4,8; I, II, and III John; Revelation)

Day 1: Walking in Love

Scripture: *1 John 4:7 – "Dear friends, let us love one another, for love comes from God. Everyone who loves has been born of God and knows God."*

Lesson: John, known as the "apostle of love," emphasized that true faith is expressed through love. Our love for others reflects our relationship with God.

Reflection: Are you showing God's love in your daily life, or do you struggle with loving difficult people?

Challenge: Make an intentional effort today to show love—through kindness, patience, or an act of service. If that is difficult, spend time meditating on God's great love for you, which continues even when you struggle to love others and be obedient to Him!

Day 2: Abiding in Christ

Scripture: *John 15:5 – "I am the vine; you are the branches. If you remain in me and I in you, you will bear much fruit; apart from me you can do nothing."*

Lesson: John recorded Jesus' teaching that staying connected to Him is the key to a fruitful life. Without Him, we accomplish nothing of eternal value.

Reflection: Are you daily abiding in Christ through prayer and His Word, or are you trying to handle life on your own?

Challenge: Set aside time today to intentionally connect with Jesus—whether through prayer, worship, or meditating on Scripture.

Day 3: Living in Truth

Scripture: *3 John 1:4 – "I have no greater joy than to hear that my children are walking in the truth."*

Lesson: John emphasized the importance of living according to God's truth, not just believing it. Truth must shape how we live.

Reflection: Are there areas in your life where you struggle to align with God's truth?

Challenge: Examine your actions today and ask, "Is this aligned with God's truth?" Make adjustments where necessary.

Day 4: From Son of Thunder to Apostle of Love

Scripture: *Mark 3:17 – "James son of Zebedee and his brother John (to them He gave the name Boanerges, which means 'sons of thunder')"*

Lesson: John was once known for his fiery, impulsive nature. But Jesus transformed him into the apostle of love. God changes hearts!

Reflection: What areas of your personality need transformation? Are you allowing Jesus to refine you?

Challenge: Identify one area of your personality where you need Christ's transforming power (anger, impatience, pride, etc.). Ask God to work in you today.

Day 5: Fixing Your Eyes on Eternity

Scripture: *Revelation 21:3-4 – "...Look! God's dwelling place is now among the people... He will wipe every tear from their eyes. There will be no more death or mourning or crying or pain..."*

Lesson: John's vision in Revelation reminds us that our hope is in Christ's eternal kingdom. Earthly struggles are temporary—our future is secure in Him.

Reflection: Are you living with eternity in mind, or are you consumed by temporary concerns?

Challenge: Shift your focus today to what truly matters. Choose to invest in things of eternal value—prayer, sharing your faith, loving others.

Final Summary: What John Teaches Us

- **Day 1:** Love is the mark of true faith—walk in love.
- **Day 2:** Abide in Christ—stay connected to Him daily.
- **Day 3:** Live in truth—let God's Word shape your life.
- **Day 4:** Let Jesus transform you—He changes hearts.
- **Day 5:** Focus on eternity—live for what truly lasts.

Life Application: Which lesson struck you the most? How will you continue to apply it to your life? Pray for a heart that abides in Christ, walks in love, and stays focused on God's eternal promises.

Chapter 47

Andrew: A Life of Humility, Evangelism, and Quiet Faithfulness

(Matthew 4,10; Mark 1,3,13; Luke 6; John 1,6,12)

Day 1: Bringing Others to Jesus

Scripture: *John 1:41-42 – "The first thing Andrew did was to find his brother Simon and tell him, 'We have found the Messiah' (that is, the Christ). And he brought him to Jesus…"*

Lesson: Andrew's first instinct after meeting Jesus was to bring his brother, Peter, to Him. He quietly led others to Christ, even those who would become more prominent than himself.

Reflection: Are you actively bringing people to Jesus, or are you keeping your faith private?

Challenge: Share Jesus with someone today—through a conversation, an invitation to church, or an encouraging message about faith.

Day 2: Seeing Possibilities Where Others See Problems

Scripture: *John 6:8-9 – "Another of His disciples, Andrew, Simon Peter's brother, spoke up, 'Here is a boy with five small barley loaves and two small fish, but how far will they go among so many?'"*

Lesson: While others saw scarcity, Andrew brought what little was available to Jesus. His faith allowed Jesus to perform a miracle.

Reflection: Do you focus more on what you lack or on what God can do with what you have?

Challenge: Offer what you have to God today, no matter how small—your time, talents, or resources. Trust Him to multiply it for His glory.

Day 3: Serving in the Background

Scripture: *John 12:21-22 – "They came to Philip, who was from Bethsaida in Galilee, with a request. 'Sir,' they said, 'we would like to see Jesus.' Philip went to tell Andrew; Andrew and Philip in turn told Jesus."*

Lesson: Andrew wasn't in the spotlight like Peter, James, or John, but he faithfully connected people to Jesus. His role was just as vital in the kingdom.

Reflection: Are you willing to serve God even if no one notices?

Challenge: Do an act of service today without seeking recognition. Serve for God's glory, not for personal praise.

Day 4: Following Jesus Without Hesitation

Scripture: *Matthew 4:19-20 – "'Come, follow me,' Jesus said, 'and I will send you out to fish for people.' At once they left their nets and followed Him."*

Lesson: Andrew and his brother Peter left everything immediately when Jesus called. They didn't hesitate or question—they obeyed.

Reflection: Is there something God is calling you to do that you've been hesitating on?

Challenge: Take a step of obedience today in something you've been delaying. Trust that God's plans are better than yours.

Day 5: Investing in One Person at a Time

Scripture: *John 1:40 – "Andrew, Simon Peter's brother, was one of the two who heard what John had said and who had followed Jesus."*

Lesson: Andrew wasn't a preacher to large crowds, but he faithfully led individuals—like Peter—to Jesus. His personal evangelism changed history.

Reflection: Are you willing to invest in just one person for Christ, even if you don't see immediate results?

Challenge: Pray for and invest in one person today. Build a relationship, share your faith, or encourage them spiritually.

Final Summary: What Andrew Teaches Us

- **Day 1:** Be a bridge to Jesus—bring others to Him.
- **Day 2:** Trust God with what you have—He can multiply it.
- **Day 3:** Serve in the background—your role matters.
- **Day 4:** Follow Jesus without hesitation—obey immediately.
- **Day 5:** Invest in one person at a time—small seeds can bring great impact.

Life Application: Which lesson resonated most with you? How will you continue to live it out? Pray for a humble and obedient heart like Andrew—faithfully serving, sharing, and trusting Jesus with the results.

Chapter 48

Thomas: A Life of Faith, Doubt, and Conviction

(Matthew 10; Mark 3; Luke 6; John 11,14,20-21)

Day 1: Following Jesus Even in Uncertainty

Scripture: *John 11:16 – "Then Thomas (also known as Didymus) said to the rest of the disciples, 'Let us also go, that we may die with him.'"*

Lesson: Thomas may be known for his doubt, but he was also deeply loyal to Jesus. He was willing to follow Him, even when it seemed dangerous.

Reflection: Are you willing to follow Jesus wholeheartedly, even when it feels risky or uncertain?

Challenge: Commit to stepping out in faith today in an area where you feel uncertain. Trust that Jesus is leading you.

Day 2: Expressing Doubts Honestly

Scripture: *John 14:5 – "Thomas said to him, 'Lord, we don't know where you are going, so how can we know the way?'"*

Lesson: Thomas wasn't afraid to ask Jesus hard questions. His doubts led to deeper understanding because he sought answers directly from Christ.

Reflection: Do you bring your doubts and questions to Jesus, or do you allow them to weaken your faith?

Challenge: If you have doubts, take time today to pray and ask God for wisdom and understanding. Seek truth through Scripture.

Day 3: Recognizing Jesus as Lord and God

Scripture: *John 20:27-28 – "Then he said to Thomas, 'Put your finger here; see my hands. Reach out your hand and put it into my side. Stop doubting and believe.' Thomas said to him, 'My Lord and my God!'"*

Lesson: When Thomas finally saw the risen Christ, he declared Jesus as "My Lord and my God!" His doubt turned into deep conviction.

Reflection: Is Jesus truly Lord of your life, or do you still hold onto doubts that keep you from fully trusting Him?

Challenge: Make a personal declaration of faith today. Speak out loud: "Jesus, You are my Lord and my God."

Day 4: Blessed Are Those Who Believe Without Seeing

Scripture: *John 20:29 – "Then Jesus told him, 'Because you have seen me, you have believed; blessed are those who have not seen and yet have believed.'"*

Lesson: Jesus reminded Thomas that true faith isn't based on sight but on trust in God's promises. We are called to believe without needing proof.

Reflection: Do you rely on feelings and experiences to sustain your faith, or do you trust in God's Word?

Challenge: Choose to trust God today, even when you don't see immediate answers to your prayers. Declare, "I believe, even when I don't see."

Day 5: Taking the Gospel to the Ends of the Earth

Scripture: *Mark 16:15 – He said to them "Go into all the world and preach the gospel to all creation."*

Lesson: Church history suggests that Thomas took the Gospel to India, spreading the message of Christ despite his early doubts. His faith led him to fulfill the Great Commission.

Reflection: Are you sharing your faith boldly, or are doubts keeping you from living out your calling?

Challenge: Share your faith with someone today—whether through a conversation, testimony, or encouragement.

Final Summary: What Thomas Teaches Us

- **Day 1:** Follow Jesus, even when it's uncertain.
- **Day 2:** Bring your doubts to Jesus—He welcomes your questions.
- **Day 3:** Declare Jesus as Lord—make Him the center of your life.
- **Day 4:** Believe without seeing—faith is trusting God beyond feelings.
- **Day 5:** Be a bold witness—take the Gospel wherever you go.

Life Application: Which lesson challenged you the most? How will you let it affect your choices moving forward? Pray for a faith that moves beyond doubt and leads to deep conviction and bold action.

Chapter 49

Philip the Apostle: Seeking Truth, Growing Faith, and Witnessing Jesus' Glory

(Matthew 10; Mark 3; Luke 6; John 1,6,12,14)

Day 1: A Sincere Seeker of Truth

Scripture: *John 1:43-45 – "The next day Jesus decided to leave for Galilee. Finding Philip, He said to him, 'Follow Me.' Philip, like Andrew and Peter, was from the town of Bethsaida. Philip found Nathanael and told him, 'We have found the one Moses wrote about in the Law, and about whom the prophets also wrote—Jesus of Nazareth, the son of Joseph.'"*

Lesson: Philip was searching for the Messiah, and when he found Jesus, he immediately shared the news with Nathanael. He was eager to follow truth wherever it led.

Reflection: Are you actively seeking truth and sharing it with others?

Challenge: Share the Good News with someone today. Tell them about Jesus and what He means to you.

Day 2: Seeking Understanding

Scripture: *John 14:8-9 – "Philip said, 'Lord, show us the Father and that will be enough for us.' Jesus answered, 'Don't you know Me, Philip, even after I have been among you such a long time? Anyone who has seen Me has seen the Father…'"*

Lesson: Philip sought deeper understanding of God, but he struggled to fully grasp Jesus' divinity. His honest questions showed his desire to know God more.

Reflection: Are you asking honest questions and seeking to understand God more deeply?

Challenge: Ask God today for greater understanding of who He is. Seek Him in Scripture and prayer with an open heart.

Day 3: Relying on Human Logic Instead of Faith

Scripture: *John 6:5,7 – "When Jesus looked up and saw a great crowd coming toward Him, He said to Philip, 'Where shall we buy bread for these people to eat?'... Philip answered Him, 'It would take more than half a year's wages to buy enough bread for each one to have a bite!'"*

Lesson: Philip focused on the practical problem rather than Jesus' power. He relied on human logic instead of faith in God's provision.

Reflection: Do you rely more on your own logic than on faith in God's power?

Challenge: Trust God with a situation that seems impossible today. Pray in faith, believing in His supernatural provision.

Day 4: Bringing Others to Jesus

Scripture: *John 12:21-22 – "They came to Philip... with a request. 'Sir,' they said, 'we would like to see Jesus.' Philip went to tell Andrew; Andrew and Philip in turn told Jesus."*

Lesson: Philip didn't have all the answers, but he knew how to bring people to Jesus. He connected seekers to the Savior.

Reflection: Are you bringing people to Jesus, even when you don't have all the answers?

Challenge: Invite someone today to learn more about Jesus—whether by inviting them to church, sharing a book, or simply starting a conversation.

Day 5: Witnessing the Glory of Christ

Scripture: *John 1:14 – "The Word became flesh and made His dwelling among us. We have seen His glory, the glory of the one and only Son, who came from the Father, full of grace and truth."*

Lesson: Philip witnessed Jesus' miracles, teachings, death, and resurrection. He saw the glory of God revealed through Christ.

Reflection: Are you recognizing God's glory and presence in your life today?

Challenge: Spend time in worship and gratitude today, acknowledging God's glory and goodness in your life.

Final Summary: What Philip the Apostle Teaches Us

- **Day 1:** Seek truth and share it with others—introduce them to Jesus.
- **Day 2:** Ask questions and seek understanding—grow in knowing God.
- **Day 3:** Trust God's power—rely on faith, not just human logic.
- **Day 4:** Connect people to Jesus—even when you don't have all the answers.
- **Day 5:** Witness and celebrate God's glory—worship with gratitude.

Life Application: Which lesson spoke to you the most? How will you carry it out moving forward? Pray for a heart like Philip's—curious, sincere, and eager to bring others to Jesus.

Chapter 50

Matthew (Levi): A Life of Grace, Transformation, and Calling

(Matthew 9-10; Mark 2-3; Luke 5-6)

Day 1: Called from a Life of Sin

Scripture: *Matthew 9:9 – "As Jesus went on from there, He saw a man named Matthew sitting at the tax collector's booth. 'Follow me,' He told him, and Matthew got up and followed Him."*

Lesson: Matthew was a tax collector—despised by society—but Jesus called him anyway. His past didn't disqualify him from God's purpose.

Reflection: Do you ever feel unworthy of God's calling? Remember that Jesus calls people not based on their past but based on His grace.

Challenge: Let go of any guilt or shame from your past. Accept God's grace and take a step forward in following Jesus today.

Day 2: Inviting Others to Meet Jesus

Scripture: *Luke 5:29 – "Then Levi held a great banquet for Jesus at his house, and a large crowd of tax collectors and others were eating with them."*

Lesson: After following Jesus, Matthew immediately invited others to experience Him. He used his influence to bring people to Christ.

Reflection: Are you inviting others to meet Jesus, or are you keeping your faith to yourself?

Challenge: Think of one person who needs to hear about Jesus. Pray for them and look for an opportunity to share your faith or invite them to church.

Day 3: Mercy Over Judgment

Scripture: *Matthew 9:12-13 – "On hearing this, Jesus said, 'It is not the healthy who need a doctor, but the sick... For I have not come to call the righteous, but sinners.'"*

Lesson: The Pharisees judged Matthew's past, but Jesus saw his potential. He reminded them that His mission was to show mercy, not condemnation.

Reflection: Do you look at people through the lens of their past mistakes, or do you see them as Jesus does?

Challenge: Extend mercy to someone today. Choose to see them with grace instead of judgment.

Day 4: Leaving Everything to Follow Jesus

Scripture: *Luke 5:28 – "And Levi got up, left everything and followed him."*

Lesson: Matthew left behind his career and wealth to follow Jesus. He understood that nothing in the world compares to a life with Christ.

Reflection: Is there anything you're holding onto that's keeping you from fully following Jesus?

Challenge: Identify one thing (a habit, fear, or distraction) that is pulling you away from Christ. Surrender it to Him today.

Day 5: Sharing the Gospel with the World

Scripture: *Matthew 28:19-20 – "Therefore go and make disciples of all nations..."*

Lesson: Matthew, once a tax collector, became a Gospel writer and a messenger of Jesus' teachings. His life was transformed into one of eternal impact.

Reflection: How are you using your life to share Jesus with others? Are you making an impact with the gifts and opportunities God has given you?

Challenge: Find a way today to share the Gospel—whether by word, action, or encouragement.

Final Summary: What Matthew Teaches Us

- **Day 1:** Jesus calls us despite our past—follow Him without hesitation.

- **Day 2:** Invite others to experience Jesus—your faith should be shared.

- **Day 3:** Show mercy instead of judgment—Jesus sees potential, not past mistakes.

- **Day 4:** Be willing to leave everything—nothing is greater than following Christ.

- **Day 5:** Use your life to spread the Gospel—God has given you a mission.

Life Application: Which lesson inspired you the most? How will you continue to practice it? Pray for a heart like Matthew's—one that follows Jesus fully, invites others in, and shares the Gospel boldly.

Chapter 51

Bartholomew (Nathanael): A Life of Sincerity, Faith, and Commitment to Christ

(Matthew 10; Mark 3; Luke 6; John 1, 21)

Day 1: Being Known by God

Scripture: *John 1:47 – "When Jesus saw Nathanael approaching, He said of him, 'Here truly is an Israelite in whom there is no deceit.'"*

Lesson: Jesus saw Nathanael's heart before they even met. He was a man of sincerity and honesty, and Jesus recognized his genuine faith.

Reflection: Do you live with sincerity before God, or do you try to appear more righteous than you really are?

Challenge: Spend time in honest prayer today. Confess any areas where you may struggle and ask God to shape your heart to be pure before Him.

Day 2: Overcoming Doubt with Faith

Scripture: *John 1:46 – "'Nazareth! Can anything good come from there?' Nathanael asked. 'Come and see,' said Philip."*

Lesson: Nathanael was skeptical at first, doubting that anything good could come from Nazareth. But he was willing to investigate for himself, and that led him to Jesus.

Reflection: Do you let doubts or preconceived ideas keep you from seeing how God is working?

Challenge: If you struggle with doubts or preconceived ideas, bring them before God. Ask Him to reveal His truth to you in a new way today.

Day 3: Recognizing Jesus as Lord

Scripture: *John 1:49 – "Then Nathanael declared, 'Rabbi, you are the Son of God; you are the king of Israel.'"*

Lesson: Once Nathanael encountered Jesus, his skepticism turned into unwavering faith. He recognized Jesus as the Messiah and boldly proclaimed it.

Reflection: Have you fully surrendered to Jesus as your Lord, or do you still hesitate in fully committing to Him?

Challenge: Make a personal declaration of faith today. Say out loud, "Jesus, You are my Lord and King." Live today with that truth in mind.

Day 4: Being a Faithful Witness

Scripture: *Matthew 10:2-3 – "These are the names of the twelve apostles: first, Simon (who is called Peter) and his brother Andrew; James son of Zebedee, and his brother John; Philip and Bartholomew..."*

Lesson: Bartholomew (Nathanael) was among the twelve disciples, faithfully following Jesus without seeking fame or recognition. His commitment was steady and enduring.

Reflection: Are you faithful to Christ even when you're not in the spotlight?

Challenge: Find a way to serve God today that no one will notice. Do it simply for His glory.

Day 5: Trusting in Greater Things to Come

Scripture: *John 1:50-51 – "Jesus said, 'You believe because I told you I saw you under the fig tree. You will see greater things than that... You will see "heaven open, and the angels of God ascending and descending on" the Son of Man.'"*

Lesson: Jesus promised Nathanael that his faith would lead him to see even greater things. A life of faith is one of continual growth and deeper revelation of God's power.

Reflection: Are you expecting greater things in your walk with Christ, or have you settled into a routine?

Challenge: Pray today for God to open your eyes to see His work in a deeper way. Expect Him to move in your life beyond what you imagine.

Final Summary: What Bartholomew (Nathanael) Teaches Us

- **Day 1:** Be sincere—God sees the heart.
- **Day 2:** Don't let doubt hold you back—seek the truth.
- **Day 3:** Declare Jesus as Lord—commit fully to Him.
- **Day 4:** Stay faithful—serve without seeking recognition.
- **Day 5:** Expect greater things—trust that God is always at work.

Life Application: Which lesson stood out to you the most? How will you continue to incorporate it in your life? Pray for a sincere faith, a bold heart, and a deeper expectation of what God will do in your life.

Chapter 52

James (Son of Zebedee): Zeal, Transformation, and Courageous Faith

(Matthew 4,10,17,26; Mark 1,3,5,9-10,14; Luke 5-6,8-9; John 21)

Day 1: Called to Follow Jesus

Scripture: *Matthew 4:21-22 – "Going on from there, He saw two other brothers, James son of Zebedee and his brother John. They were in a boat with their father Zebedee, preparing their nets. Jesus called them, and immediately they left the boat and their father and followed Him."*

Lesson: James and John left everything behind to follow Jesus immediately. Their response shows their willingness to obey without hesitation.

Reflection: Are you willing to leave behind comfort, plans, or distractions to fully follow Jesus?

Challenge: Identify one thing that is holding you back from fully following Jesus and take a step today to surrender it. Don't delay.

Day 2: From a Son of Thunder to a Servant of Christ

Scripture: *Mark 3:17 – "James son of Zebedee and his brother John (to them He gave the name Boanerges, which means 'sons of thunder')."*

Lesson: Like his brother, James had a fiery, impulsive personality. But Jesus transformed his zeal into a passion for the Gospel. God shapes us for His purposes.

Reflection: Are there areas in your personality that need refining by Jesus?

Challenge: Ask God to take your strengths and weaknesses and use them for His glory. Seek to be bold in love, not just in passion.

Day 3: Seeking Greatness in the Right Way

Scripture: *Mark 10:35-37 – "Then James and John, the sons of Zebedee, came to Him. 'Teacher,' they said, 'we want You to do for us whatever we ask.' 'What do you want me to do for you?' He asked. They replied, 'Let one of us sit at Your right and the other at Your left in Your glory.'"*

Lesson: James and John wanted positions of power, but Jesus taught that true greatness comes through humility and serving others.

Reflection: Are you seeking recognition and status, or are you pursuing true greatness through servanthood?

Challenge: Serve someone today without expecting anything in return.

Day 4: Facing Persecution Boldly

Scripture: *John 15:20 – "Remember what I told you: 'A servant is not greater than his master.' If they persecuted me, they will persecute you also..."*

Lesson: James was the first apostle to be martyred for his faith. His boldness for Christ cost him his life, but he remained faithful to the end.

Reflection: Are you willing to stand for your faith even when it's difficult?

Challenge: Pray for courage to stand firm in your beliefs, even in the face of opposition.

Day 5: Leaving a Legacy of Bold Faith

Scripture: *Acts 12:1-2 – "It was about this time that King Herod arrested some who belonged to the church, intending to persecute them. He had James, the brother of John, put to death with the sword."*

Lesson: James may not have lived long after Jesus' resurrection, but his impact was great. His boldness and unwavering faith helped build the early church.

Reflection: What kind of spiritual legacy are you leaving behind?

Challenge: Think of one way you can leave a lasting spiritual impact—whether mentoring someone, sharing your testimony, or committing to bold faith. Take action today.

Final Summary: What James (Son of Zebedee) Teaches Us

- **Day 1:** Follow Jesus wholeheartedly—leave behind anything that holds you back.

- **Day 2:** Let Jesus transform your strengths and weaknesses for His purpose.

- **Day 3:** Seek true greatness by serving others, not seeking recognition.

- **Day 4:** Stand firm in faith, even in persecution.

- **Day 5:** Live in a way that leaves a bold, faithful legacy.

Life Application: Which lesson resonates with you the most? How will you continue to apply it moving forward? Pray for a heart that follows Jesus fully, serves with humility, and stands boldly for the Gospel.

Chapter 53

Judas Iscariot: Lost Potential, Betrayal, and the Consequences of Unrepentant Sin

(Matthew 10,26-27; Mark 3,14; Luke 6,22; John 6,12-13,17-18)

Day 1: Chosen Yet Uncommitted

Scripture: *Luke 6:13, 16 – "When morning came, He called His disciples to Him and chose twelve of them, whom He also designated apostles:... and Judas Iscariot, who became a traitor."*

Lesson: Judas was chosen by Jesus as one of the twelve apostles, given the same opportunities as Peter, John, and the others. Yet, despite his calling, his heart was never fully committed.

Reflection: Are you following Jesus outwardly but holding back commitment in your heart?

Challenge: Examine your heart today. Ask God to reveal any area where you're half-heartedly following Him. Surrender fully to Jesus' lordship.

Day 2: Love of Money Leading to Corruption

Scripture: *John 12:4-6 – "But one of His disciples, Judas Iscariot, who was later to betray Him, objected, 'Why wasn't this perfume sold and the money given to the poor? It was worth* *a year's wages.' He did not say this because he cared about the poor but because he was a thief; as keeper of the money bag, he used to help himself to what was put into it."*

Lesson: Judas' love of money opened the door to sin. His hidden greed and dishonesty led to greater corruption and ultimately betrayal.

Reflection: Is there something you're holding onto that's leading you away from Jesus—money, power, pride, or worldly desires?

Challenge: Identify any area where materialism or selfish ambition has taken root. Confess it to God and choose generosity and integrity today.

Day 3: Betraying Jesus for Temporary Gain

Scripture: *Matthew 26:14-16 – "Then one of the Twelve—the one called Judas Iscariot—went to the chief priests and asked, 'What are you willing to give me if I deliver Him over to you?' So they counted out for him thirty pieces of silver. From then on Judas watched for an opportunity to hand him over."*

Lesson: Judas traded his relationship with Jesus for temporary gain—thirty pieces of silver. He valued worldly wealth over eternal life.

Reflection: Are you compromising your faith or values for temporary pleasures or gains?

Challenge: Identify one area where you're compromising for temporary satisfaction. Confess your sin and choose to honor God instead, valuing your relationship with Jesus above all.

Day 4: Regret Without True Repentance

Scripture: *Matthew 27:3-5 – "When Judas, who had betrayed Him, saw that Jesus was condemned, he was seized with remorse and returned the thirty pieces of silver to the chief priests and the elders. 'I have sinned,' he said, 'for I have betrayed innocent blood'... Then he went away and hanged himself."*

Lesson: Judas felt remorse but didn't seek forgiveness from God. His regret led to despair instead of redemption. True repentance involves turning to Jesus for mercy and restoration.

Reflection: Are you holding onto guilt or shame without seeking Jesus' forgiveness and healing?

Challenge: If you're struggling with guilt or shame, bring it to Jesus today. Confess your sins, receive His forgiveness, and walk in freedom.

Day 5: The Consequences of Unrepentant Sin

Scripture: *Acts 1:24-25 – "Then they prayed, 'Lord, You know everyone's heart. Show us which of these two You have chosen to take over this apostolic ministry, which Judas left to go where he belongs.'"*

Lesson: Judas lost his position and destiny because of unrepentant sin. His potential was wasted because he chose betrayal over loyalty and despair over repentance.

Reflection: Are you allowing sin or disobedience to rob you of God's purpose and calling in your life?

Challenge: Reflect on any area of unrepentant sin. Seek forgiveness today and recommit to God's purpose for your life. Don't let sin rob you of your destiny.

Final Summary: What Judas Iscariot Teaches Us

- **Day 1:** Commitment matters—outward following is not enough; your heart must be fully surrendered.

- **Day 2:** Guard your heart—greed and selfish ambition lead to corruption.

- **Day 3:** Value eternal life over temporary gain—don't compromise your faith.

- **Day 4:** Seek true repentance—remorse without turning to Jesus leads to despair.

- **Day 5:** Don't waste your potential—sin and disobedience can rob you of your calling.

Life Application: Which lesson challenged you the most? How will you live it out? Pray for a heart that is fully committed to Jesus, valuing Him above all worldly gains, and seeking true repentance and restoration.

Chapter 54

Simon the Zealot, Judas (Thaddeus), and James (Son of Alphaeus): Humble Service, Faithfulness, and Quiet Obedience

(Matthew 10; Mark 3; Luke 6; John 14)

Day 1: Chosen and Called by Jesus

Scripture: *Luke 6:13, 15 – "When morning came, He called His disciples to Him and chose twelve of them, whom He also designated apostles:... James son of Alphaeus, Simon who was called the Zealot, Judas son of James, and Judas Iscariot, who became a traitor."*

Lesson: Although little is written about them, Simon the Zealot, Judas (Thaddeus), and James (Son of Alphaeus) were personally chosen by Jesus to be His apostles. Their significance wasn't in fame but in their calling and faithfulness.

Reflection: Do you find your worth in recognition, or do you rest in the fact that Jesus has chosen and called you for His purpose?

Challenge: Reflect on your calling today. Rest in the truth that you are chosen by God, even if no one notices your work or service.

Day 2: Serving Quietly Without Recognition

Scripture: *Matthew 10:2-4 – "These are the names of the twelve apostles: first, Simon (who is called Peter) and his brother Andrew... James son of Alphaeus, and Thaddeus; Simon the Zealot and Judas Iscariot, who betrayed him."*

Lesson: Unlike Peter or John, these three apostles served quietly without seeking attention. They were faithful in their calling, showing that impact isn't always measured by visibility.

Reflection: Are you willing to serve God faithfully, even if no one sees or acknowledges your work?

Challenge: Serve someone today without seeking recognition. Let your service be an act of worship to God alone.

Day 3: Faithfulness in the Background

Scripture: *John 6:67-69 – "'You do not want to leave too, do you?' Jesus asked the Twelve. Simon Peter answered Him, 'Lord, to whom shall we go? You have the words of eternal life. We have come to believe and to know that You are the Holy One of God.'"*

Lesson: Even though they weren't in the spotlight, Simon the Zealot, Judas (Thaddeus), and James (Son of Alphaeus) stayed faithful when others turned away. They were loyal disciples, committed to following Jesus.

Reflection: Are you faithful to Jesus even when you're in the background and no one notices your commitment?

Challenge: Commit to faithfulness today. Spend time with Jesus in prayer and Scripture, even if no one sees or praises your devotion.

Day 4: Unity Despite Differences

Scripture: *Mark 3:18 – "...Andrew, Philip, Bartholomew, Matthew, Thomas, James son of Alphaeus, Thaddaeus, Simon the Zealot..."*

Lesson: Simon was a Zealot (a Jewish political revolutionary), while Matthew was a tax collector (seen as a traitor to the Jewish people). Yet, they were united as followers of Jesus. True discipleship transcends differences.

Reflection: Do you maintain unity with other believers, even when they come from different backgrounds or have different views?

Challenge: Seek unity today by reaching out to someone different from you. Show love, respect, and the bond of Christ's love.

Day 5: Leaving a Legacy of Faith and Love

Scripture: *John 15:13 – "Greater love has no one than this: to lay down one's life for one's friends."*

Lesson: Although little is recorded about their ministries, church tradition holds that Simon, Judas (Thaddeus), and James (Son of Alphaeus) were faithful in spreading the Gospel and died as martyrs. Their legacy was built on obedience and perseverance.

Reflection: Are you leaving a legacy of faith, love, and obedience, even if your name isn't remembered?

Challenge: Invest in someone's spiritual growth today—mentor, encourage, or pray for them. Leave a legacy that impacts eternity.

Final Summary: What Simon the Zealot, Judas (Thaddeus), and James (Son of Alphaeus) Teach Us

- **Day 1:** Rest in being chosen—your worth is in God's calling, not recognition.
- **Day 2:** Serve quietly—faithfulness matters more than visibility.
- **Day 3:** Stay faithful—commit to following Jesus, even in the background.
- **Day 4:** Seek unity—love others beyond differences.
- **Day 5:** Leave a legacy—invest in eternity through obedience, love, and discipleship.

Life Application: Which lesson spoke to you the most? How will you let it affect your decisions moving forward? Pray for a heart like Simon, Judas, and James—humble, faithful, and committed to Jesus, regardless of recognition or fame.

Chapter 55

Lazarus: A Life of Resurrection, Faith, and Trust in God's Timing

(John 11-12)

Day 1: Trusting God Even When He Delays

Scripture: *John 11:6 – "So when He heard that Lazarus was sick, He stayed where He was two more days."*

Lesson: Jesus intentionally delayed going to Lazarus, even though He loved him. God's timing is often different from ours, but it is always perfect.

Reflection: Do you trust God even when He seems to delay answering your prayers?

Challenge: Surrender any area of your life where you're waiting on God. Trust that His timing is best.

Day 2: Jesus Weeps With Us

Scripture: *John 11:35 – "Jesus wept."*

Lesson: Even though Jesus knew He would raise Lazarus, He still wept with those mourning. He cares deeply about our pain.

Reflection: Do you allow yourself to bring your grief and struggles to Jesus, knowing He understands and cares?

Challenge: Spend time in prayer today, sharing your burdens or pain with Jesus. Let Him weep with you and comfort you.

Day 3: God's Power is Greater Than Death

Scripture: *John 11:43-44 – "When He had said this, Jesus called in a loud voice, 'Lazarus, come out!' The dead man came out..."*

Lesson: Jesus demonstrated His power over death, proving that nothing is beyond His ability to restore and heal.

Reflection: Are there areas in your life that feel hopeless or "dead"? Do you believe Jesus can bring new life to them?

Challenge: Pray for God to restore any situation in your life that feels dead or beyond hope.

Day 4: Responding to God's Call

Scripture: *John 11:44 – "The dead man came out, his hands and feet wrapped with strips of linen, and a cloth around his face. Jesus said to them, 'Take off the grave clothes and let him go.'"*

Lesson: Lazarus had to respond to Jesus' call to step into new life. God calls us to walk out of our past and into His freedom.

Reflection: Are you holding onto things that keep you from fully walking in God's freedom?

Challenge: Let go of anything that is keeping you from fully following Jesus—fear, sin, or past hurts.

Day 5: Living as a Testimony

Scripture: *John 12:10-11 – "So the chief priests made plans to kill Lazarus as well, for on account of him many of the Jews were going over to Jesus and believing in Him."*

Lesson: Lazarus' resurrection was so powerful that people turned to Jesus because of his testimony. A transformed life points others to Christ.

Reflection: Is your life a testimony that draws others to Jesus?

Challenge: Share a part of your testimony today—whether through conversation, social media, or an act of love.

Final Summary: What Lazarus Teaches Us

- **Day 1:** Trust God's timing—He is never late.

- **Day 2:** Jesus cares about your pain—bring your burdens to Him.

- **Day 3:** Nothing is beyond God's power—He can restore anything.

- **Day 4:** Step out of the past—walk in new life with Christ.

- **Day 5:** Live as a testimony—your life should point others to Jesus.

Life Application: Which lesson do you need to put into practice the most? How will you do that going forward? Pray for a heart that trusts God, walks in new life, and boldly shares His transforming power.

Chapter 56

Zacchaeus: Seeking Jesus, Repentance, and Radical Transformation

(Luke 19)

Day 1: Seeking Jesus Despite Obstacles

Scripture: *Luke 19:3-4 – "He wanted to see who Jesus was, but because he was short he could not see over the crowd. So he ran ahead and climbed a sycamore-fig tree to see Him, since Jesus was coming that way."*

Lesson: Zacchaeus didn't let his limitations stop him from seeking Jesus. His curiosity and determination led him to find a way despite the obstacles.

Reflection: Are there obstacles—doubts, fears, or distractions—that are keeping you from seeking Jesus fully?

Challenge: Identify one obstacle that's hindering your relationship with Jesus. Take a step today to overcome it—whether through prayer, surrender, or intentional focus on God.

Day 2: Jesus Sees and Calls You by Name

Scripture: *Luke 19:5 – "When Jesus reached the spot, he looked up and said to him, 'Zacchaeus, come down immediately. I must stay at your house today.'"*

Lesson: Jesus saw Zacchaeus before Zacchaeus saw Him. He called him by name and invited Himself into Zacchaeus' life, showing that God knows us personally and seeks a relationship with us.

Reflection: Do you realize that Jesus knows you by name and desires to be close to you, no matter who you are or where you've been?

Challenge: Spend time today reflecting on the fact that Jesus sees you and knows you fully. Talk to Him openly in prayer, knowing He desires to be near you.

Day 3: Welcoming Jesus with Joy

Scripture: *Luke 19:6 – "So he came down at once and welcomed him gladly."*

Lesson: Zacchaeus didn't hesitate—he welcomed Jesus with joy. Despite his past as a tax collector, he received Jesus with an open heart.

Reflection: Are you welcoming Jesus into every area of your life, or are you keeping parts of your heart closed off?

Challenge: Invite Jesus into every area of your life today, especially the parts you've been hesitant to surrender. Welcome Him with joy and gratitude.

Day 4: Repentance and Radical Transformation

Scripture: *Luke 19:8 – "But Zacchaeus stood up and said to the Lord, 'Look, Lord! Here and now I give half of my possessions to the poor, and if I have cheated anybody out of anything, I will pay back four times the amount.'"*

Lesson: Encountering Jesus led Zacchaeus to repentance and radical change. He didn't just confess—he took action to make things right, showing genuine transformation.

Reflection: Are there areas in your life where you need to repent and make things right? Are you willing to change, even if it's costly?

Challenge: Examine your heart today and ask God to reveal any area needing repentance. Take a practical step toward making things right.

Day 5: Salvation and Restoration

Scripture: *Luke 19:9-10 – "Jesus said to him, 'Today salvation has come to this house, because this man, too, is a son of Abraham. For the Son of Man came to seek and to save the lost.'"*

Lesson: Jesus publicly affirmed Zacchaeus' faith and declared his salvation, restoring him to his community and identity as a son of Abraham. God's grace restores what was lost.

Reflection: Do you believe that Jesus' salvation and restoration are available to you, regardless of your past? Do you trust in your identity as a son of God?

Challenge: Accept God's grace today. Let go of any shame or guilt and walk confidently in the identity Jesus has given you as a son of God.

Final Summary: What Zacchaeus Teaches Us

- **Day 1:** Seek Jesus despite obstacles—don't let anything hold you back.
- **Day 2:** Jesus sees and knows you personally—He calls you by name.
- **Day 3:** Welcome Jesus with joy—surrender every area of your life to Him.
- **Day 4:** True repentance brings transformation—make things right.
- **Day 5:** Jesus' salvation restores—walk confidently in your new identity.

Life Application: Which lesson struck you the most? How will you carry it out going forward? Pray for a heart like Zacchaeus—one that seeks Jesus fully, repents genuinely, and welcomes His transforming grace with joy.

Chapter 57

Nicodemus: A Journey from Curiosity to Courageous Faith

(John 3,7,19)

Day 1: Seeking Jesus in the Night

Scripture: *John 3:1-2 – "Now there was a Pharisee, a man named Nicodemus who was a member of the Jewish ruling council. He came to Jesus at night and said, 'Rabbi, we know that you are a teacher who has come from God. For no one could perform the signs you are doing if God were not with him.'"*

Lesson: Nicodemus was curious but cautious. He sought Jesus at night, showing his desire to understand while fearing public opinion. Even in his uncertainty, he was willing to learn.

Reflection: Are you seeking Jesus even when you have questions or doubts? Are you willing to learn, even if you don't have all the answers?

Challenge: Bring your questions to Jesus today. Spend time in prayer and the Scriptures, seeking understanding and wisdom from Him.

Day 2: The Mystery of Being Born Again

Scripture: *John 3:3 – "Jesus replied, 'Very truly I tell you, no one can see the kingdom of God unless they are born again.'"*

Lesson: Nicodemus struggled to understand spiritual rebirth. Jesus revealed that entering God's kingdom requires a transformation only the Holy Spirit can bring.

Reflection: Have you experienced the new birth that comes from trusting in Christ, or are you relying on religious knowledge and good deeds?

Challenge: Reflect on your relationship with Jesus. If you've never surrendered your life to Him, consider doing so today. If you have, thank Him for your new life in Christ and lean into the transforming power of the Holy Spirit.

Day 3: Wrestling with Understanding

Scripture: *John 3:9-10* – *"'How can this be?' Nicodemus asked. 'You are Israel's teacher,' said Jesus, 'and do you not understand these things?'"*

Lesson: Nicodemus was an educated religious leader but struggled to grasp spiritual truths. Jesus challenged him to move beyond intellectual knowledge to spiritual understanding.

Reflection: Are you growing in spiritual wisdom, or are you only accumulating religious knowledge?

Challenge: Ask God today for spiritual insight and understanding. Seek to know Him more deeply, not just intellectually.

Day 4: Defending Jesus in the Midst of Opposition

Scripture: *John 7:50-51* – *"Nicodemus, who had gone to Jesus earlier and who was one of their own number, asked, 'Does our law condemn a man without first hearing him to find out what he has been doing?'"*

Lesson: Nicodemus stood up for justice even though it meant he had to go against popular opinion. He maintained his integrity even in the face of opposition.

Reflection: Are you willing to pursue justice and maintain integrity, even if it costs you your reputation or popularity?

Challenge: Ask God if there is any area of your life where you have neglected to stand up for justice or truth in order to avoid conflict or be accepted. Ask for forgiveness and take steps to make it right.

Day 5: Boldly Following Jesus

Scripture: *John 19:39 – "He was accompanied by Nicodemus, the man who earlier had visited Jesus at night. Nicodemus brought a mixture of myrrh and aloes, about seventy-five pounds."*

Lesson: Nicodemus went from visiting Jesus in secret to publicly honoring Him at His burial. His faith grew from curiosity to courageous devotion.

Reflection: Are you willing to publicly follow Jesus, even if it means risking your reputation or facing criticism?

Challenge: Take a public step of faith today—whether through sharing your testimony, standing for biblical truth, or serving others in Jesus' name.

Final Summary: What Nicodemus Teaches Us

- **Day 1:** Seek Jesus even with questions—curiosity can lead to faith.
- **Day 2:** Be born again—spiritual transformation is essential.
- **Day 3:** Move from knowledge to relationship—seek spiritual wisdom.
- **Day 4:** Stand for justice and truth—maintain integrity even when it's unpopular.
- **Day 5:** Boldly follow Jesus—let your faith grow from curiosity to courage.

Life Application: Which lesson resonated with you the most? How will you practice it moving forward? Pray for a heart like Nicodemus—one that seeks Jesus, grows in faith, and boldly stands for truth.

Chapter 58

Jairus: A Journey of Desperation, Faith, and Trusting in Jesus' Timing

(Matthew 9; Mark 5; Luke 8)

Day 1: Desperation Drives Us to Jesus

Scripture: *Mark 5:22-23 – "Then one of the synagogue leaders, named Jairus, came, and when he saw Jesus, he fell at His feet. He pleaded earnestly with Him, 'My little daughter is dying. Please come and put Your hands on her so that she will be healed and live.'"*

Lesson: Jairus was a respected leader, yet his desperation for his daughter's life drove him to fall at Jesus' feet, humbling himself and seeking help. Desperation can lead us to deeper faith.

Reflection: Are you willing to humble yourself before Jesus, bringing Him your deepest needs and fears?

Challenge: Bring your most urgent need or fear to Jesus today. Humble yourself in prayer, trusting Him to move in your situation.

Day 2: Waiting in Faith When Delays Happen

Scripture: *Mark 5:35 – "While Jesus was still speaking, some people came from the house of Jairus, the synagogue leader. 'Your daughter is dead,' they said. 'Why bother the teacher anymore?'"*

Lesson: On the way to Jairus' house, Jesus was interrupted by healing the woman with the issue of blood. The delay seemed like a setback, but Jesus' timing was perfect.

Reflection: Do you trust Jesus' timing, even when delays seem to make things worse?

Challenge: If you're waiting on God to move, choose to trust His timing today. Surrender your timeline and ask for faith to believe that He's working behind the scenes.

Day 3: Overcoming Fear with Faith

Scripture: *Mark 5:36 – "Overhearing what they said, Jesus told him, 'Don't be afraid; just believe.'"*

Lesson: When Jairus heard the news of his daughter's death, fear and hopelessness tried to take over. But Jesus challenged him to replace fear with faith.

Reflection: Are you allowing fear to control your life, or are you choosing faith in Jesus' words and promises?

Challenge: Identify one fear you're facing today. Speak faith over it by declaring God's promises in Scripture. Choose to believe instead of fearing.

Day 4: Trusting Jesus Behind Closed Doors

Scripture: *Mark 5:40 – "But they laughed at him. After He put them all out, He took the child's father and mother and the disciples who were with Him, and went in where the child was."*

Lesson: Jesus didn't allow the crowd's doubt to enter the room. He invited only a few to witness the miracle, teaching us that sometimes faith requires closing the door to doubt and negativity.

Reflection: Are you letting others' doubts or negativity weaken your faith?

Challenge: Close the door to negativity today. Surround yourself with people who will encourage your faith and pray with you.

Day 5: Witnessing Resurrection Power

Scripture: *Mark 5:41-42 – "He took her by the hand and said to her, 'Talitha koum!' (which means 'Little girl, I say to you, get up!'). Immediately the girl stood up and began to walk around... they were completely astonished."*

Lesson: Jairus' faith led him to witness Jesus' resurrection power. What seemed impossible became a testimony of God's authority over life and death.

Reflection: Are you expecting Jesus to bring life and restoration to seemingly impossible situations?

Challenge: Pray boldly for a miracle today. Ask Jesus to bring resurrection power to any dead or hopeless area in your life.

Final Summary: What Jairus Teaches Us

- **Day 1:** Desperation leads to deeper faith—come to Jesus with your needs.
- **Day 2:** Trust God's timing—delays are not denials.
- **Day 3:** Choose faith over fear—believe in Jesus' promises.
- **Day 4:** Close the door to doubt—surround yourself with faith.
- **Day 5:** Expect resurrection power—Jesus can restore anything.

Life Application: Which lesson stood out to you the most? How will you continue to apply it in your life? Pray for faith like Jairus—bold enough to ask, patient enough to wait, and strong enough to believe.

Chapter 59

The Centurion: A Life of Humility, Faith, and Trust in Jesus' Authority

(Matthew 8; Luke 7)

Day 1: Humility Before Greatness

Scripture: *Matthew 8:5 – "When Jesus had entered Capernaum, a centurion came to Him, asking for help."*

Lesson: The centurion was a man of authority, yet he humbled himself to seek Jesus' help for his servant. His humility was the first step to experiencing Jesus' power.

Reflection: Are you willing to humble yourself before Jesus, acknowledging your need for His help?

Challenge: Identify one area of your life where you need Jesus' intervention. Humble yourself today by praying and surrendering that area to Him.

Day 2: Compassion Beyond Status

Scripture: *Matthew 8:6 – "'Lord,' he said. 'my servant lies at home paralyzed, suffering terribly.'"*

Lesson: The centurion cared deeply for his servant, showing compassion despite the social hierarchy. True faith is marked by love and empathy.

Reflection: Do you show compassion and care for those who may be "below" you in status or position?

Challenge: Show kindness and compassion today to someone who may be overlooked or undervalued. Reflect Christ's love through your actions.

Day 3: Faith in Jesus' Authority

Scripture: *Matthew 8:8-9 – "The centurion replied, 'Lord, I do not deserve to have You come under my roof. But just say the word, and my servant will be healed. For I myself am a man under authority, with soldiers under me. I tell this one, "Go," and he goes; and that one, "Come," and he comes...'"*

Lesson: The centurion understood authority. He believed that Jesus' word alone had the power to heal, demonstrating profound faith in Christ's authority.

Reflection: Do you trust in the power of Jesus' word, or do you need physical evidence to believe?

Challenge: Speak God's promises over your life today. Declare His authority and trust that His word is enough.

Day 4: Astonishing Jesus with Faith

Scripture: *Matthew 8:10 – "When Jesus heard this, He was amazed and said to those following Him, 'Truly I tell you, I have not found anyone in Israel with such great faith.'"*

Lesson: The centurion's faith amazed Jesus. It wasn't based on religious background or status but on trust in who Jesus is.

Reflection: Is your faith bold enough to trust Jesus completely, no matter the situation?

Challenge: Pray boldly today for a miracle or breakthrough. Believe without doubt, knowing Jesus is able.

Day 5: Witnessing the Power of the Word

Scripture: *Matthew 8:13 – "Then Jesus said to the centurion, 'Go! Let it be done just as you believed it would.' And his servant was healed at that moment."*

Lesson: Because of his faith, the centurion witnessed the power of Jesus' word. His servant was healed instantly, demonstrating that faith activates God's power.

Reflection: Are you expecting God's word to work powerfully in your life?

Challenge: Seek God's help today and wait for Him to answer. While you wait, speak God's promises over your circumstances. Believe in the power of His word and expect to see His power at work.

Final Summary: What The Centurion Teaches Us

- **Day 1:** Humble yourself before Jesus—acknowledge your need for Him.

- **Day 2:** Show compassion—faith is expressed through love.

- **Day 3:** Trust Jesus' authority—His word is enough.

- **Day 4:** Have bold faith—trust Jesus completely.

- **Day 5:** Expect the power of the Word—God's promises are true.

Life Application: Which lesson challenged you the most? How will you incorporate it in your life moving forward? Pray for faith like the centurion—bold, humble, and fully trusting in Jesus' authority.

Chapter 60

The Thief on the Cross: A Journey of Repentance, Faith, and Grace

(Matthew 27; Mark 1; Luke 23)

Day 1: Recognizing Our Sinfulness

Scripture: *Luke 23:39-40 – "One of the criminals who hung there hurled insults at Him: 'Aren't you the Messiah? Save yourself and us!' But the other criminal rebuked him. 'Don't you fear God,' he said, 'since you are under the same sentence?'"*

Lesson: The repentant thief recognized his own sinfulness and acknowledged that he deserved his punishment. True repentance begins with recognizing our need for a Savior.

Reflection: Are you honest with yourself about your need for God's forgiveness, or do you justify or minimize your sins?

Challenge: Take time today to reflect on areas where you need forgiveness. Humbly confess your sins to God, trusting in His mercy.

Day 2: Acknowledging Christ's Innocence and Lordship

Scripture: *Luke 23:41 – "We are punished justly, for we are getting what our deeds deserve. But this man has done nothing wrong."*

Lesson: The thief recognized Jesus' innocence and holiness. He saw Jesus as more than just a man—he saw Him as the sinless Savior.

Reflection: Do you see Jesus as the perfect, sinless Savior who bore your sins on the cross?

Challenge: Spend time in worship today, acknowledging Jesus' holiness and thanking Him for taking your place on the cross.

Day 3: A Simple Yet Powerful Prayer of Faith

Scripture: *Luke 23:42 – "Then he said, 'Jesus, remember me when You come into Your kingdom.'"*

Lesson: With a simple plea, the thief expressed faith in Jesus as King and trusted Him for salvation. His faith wasn't based on religious knowledge but on a heart that believed.

Reflection: Do you approach Jesus with simple, childlike faith, or do you overcomplicate your relationship with Him?

Challenge: Pray a simple prayer of faith today. Speak to Jesus from your heart, trusting Him completely with your life.

Day 4: Receiving Grace at the Last Moment

Scripture: *Luke 23:43 – "Jesus answered him, 'Truly I tell you, today you will be with Me in paradise.'"*

Lesson: Even in his final moments, the thief received grace and the promise of eternal life. It's never too late to turn to Jesus—His grace is always available.

Reflection: Do you truly believe that God's grace is sufficient, no matter how late or undeserved it may seem?

Challenge: If you've been holding back because of guilt or shame, accept God's grace today. Let go of your past and receive His forgiveness.

Day 5: Assurance of Salvation

Scripture: *John 10:28 – "I give them eternal life, and they shall never perish; no one will snatch them out of My hand."*

Lesson: Jesus gave the thief assurance of his salvation, and He does the same for us. Once we place our faith in Christ, we are secure in His promise of eternal life.

Reflection: Are you confident in your salvation, or do you struggle with doubt and insecurity?

Challenge: Make sure your faith is placed in the person of Jesus Christ and not a religious idea. Life with Jesus is about Him knowing you and you knowing Him in a personal way, not just knowing of or about Him. It is about relationship. If you are in that relationship, rest in the assurance of God's promises today. Write down or memorize Scriptures about salvation and meditate on them.

Final Summary: What The Thief on the Cross Teaches Us

- **Day 1:** Recognize your need for forgiveness—confess your sins to God.

- **Day 2:** Acknowledge Jesus as the sinless Savior—worship Him.

- **Day 3:** Pray with simple faith—trust Jesus with your life.

- **Day 4:** Receive God's grace—it's never too late to turn to Him.

- **Day 5:** Rest in the assurance of salvation—Jesus holds you securely.

Life Application: Which lesson spoke to you the most? How will you continue to live it out? Pray for a heart that fully trusts in Jesus' grace, forgiveness, and promise of eternal life.

Chapter 61

Simon of Cyrene: Unexpected Purpose, Humble Service, and Carrying the Cross

(Matthew 27; Mark 15; Luke 23)

Day 1: An Unexpected Encounter with Jesus

Scripture: *Luke 23:26 – "As the soldiers led him away, they seized Simon from Cyrene, who was on his way in from the country, and put the cross on him and made him carry it behind Jesus."*

Lesson: Simon didn't plan to meet Jesus that day. He was just passing by, yet he was chosen to carry the cross. God often interrupts our plans to fulfill His purpose.

Reflection: Are you open to God interrupting your plans for a greater purpose?

Challenge: Be flexible today. Allow God to interrupt your schedule or routine and be open to unexpected opportunities to serve Him.

Day 2: Carrying the Cross Behind Jesus

Scripture: *Luke 23:26 – "...and made him carry it behind Jesus."*

Lesson: Simon literally followed Jesus while carrying the cross. It was a physical burden, but also a symbolic act of discipleship. We are called to follow Jesus by carrying our own crosses.

Reflection: Are you willing to carry your cross and follow Jesus, even when it's difficult or inconvenient?

Challenge: Identify one burden or challenge you're facing today. Choose to carry it with faith, trusting that Jesus walks before you.

Day 3: Serving Without Recognition

Scripture: *Matthew 27:32 – "As they were going out, they met a man from Cyrene, named Simon, and they forced him to carry the cross."*

Lesson: Simon's act of service wasn't voluntary, and he didn't receive recognition. Yet his obedience was essential in God's plan. True service often goes unnoticed but is valuable in God's kingdom.

Reflection: Are you willing to serve God even when no one notices or praises you?

Challenge: Do an act of service today in secret—help someone, pray for someone, or give generously without seeking recognition.

Day 4: Transforming an Unwanted Task into Purpose

Scripture: *Mark 15:21 – "A certain man from Cyrene, Simon, the father of Alexander and Rufus, was passing by on his way in from the country, and they forced him to carry the cross."*

Lesson: What seemed like an inconvenience or burden became Simon's greatest purpose. He helped carry the cross of the Savior of the world. God turns our burdens into blessings.

Reflection: Are you seeing your challenges as inconveniences, or as opportunities for God to work through you?

Challenge: Reframe one challenge or "burden" today. Choose to see it as an opportunity for God to reveal His purpose and glory through it.

Day 5: Impacting Future Generations

Scripture: *Mark 15:21 – "...Simon, the father of Alexander and Rufus..."*

Lesson: Simon's experience impacted his family. His sons, Alexander and Rufus, witnessed their father's service. Our faithfulness today influences future generations.

Reflection: Are you living in a way that leaves a legacy of faith for those who come after you?

Challenge: Pray today for the next generation—your children, relatives, or young people in your community. Ask God to use your life to influence them for Christ.

Final Summary: What Simon of Cyrene Teaches Us

- **Day 1:** Be open to God's interruptions—He has a purpose for you.
- **Day 2:** Carry your cross—follow Jesus, even through challenges.
- **Day 3:** Serve humbly—God values obedience, not recognition.
- **Day 4:** See burdens as blessings—God transforms inconveniences into purpose.
- **Day 5:** Leave a legacy of faith—your obedience impacts future generations.

Life Application: Which lesson do you need to put into practice the most? How will you do that going forward? Pray for a heart like Simon's—willing to carry the cross, serve humbly, and leave a legacy of faith.

Chapter 62

Bartimaeus: Persistent Faith, Boldness, and Receiving Sight from Jesus

(Mark 10; Luke 18)

Day 1: Recognizing Jesus as the Messiah

Scripture: *Mark 10:47 – "When he heard that it was Jesus of Nazareth, he began to shout, 'Jesus, Son of David, have mercy on me!'"*

Lesson: Bartimaeus recognized Jesus as the "Son of David," a Messianic title. Even in his blindness, he saw who Jesus truly was— the promised Savior.

Reflection: Do you recognize Jesus as the Messiah and Savior of your life, or do you see Him only as a teacher or miracle worker?

Challenge: Spend time today in worship, declaring Jesus as your Lord and Savior. Acknowledge His authority and divinity.

Day 2: Persistent Faith Amid Opposition

Scripture: *Mark 10:48 – "Many rebuked him and told him to be quiet, but he shouted all the more, 'Son of David, have mercy on me!'"*

Lesson: Despite being told to be silent, Bartimaeus persisted in calling out to Jesus. His faith wasn't deterred by opposition or criticism.

Reflection: Are you persistent in seeking Jesus, even when others try to discourage you?

Challenge: Pray persistently today for something you've been seeking from God. Don't let doubt or discouragement stop you.

Day 3: Boldness to Ask for the Impossible

Scripture: *Mark 10:51 – "'What do you want Me to do for you?' Jesus asked him. The blind man said, 'Rabbi, I want to see.'"*

Lesson: Bartimaeus didn't hesitate or limit his request. He boldly asked Jesus for his sight, demonstrating faith in Jesus' power to do the impossible.

Reflection: Are you asking God boldly for the desires of your heart, or are you afraid to ask for the impossible?

Challenge: Ask God boldly for a miracle or breakthrough today. Don't hold back—trust in His power and goodness.

Day 4: Leaving Behind the Old Life

Scripture: *Mark 10:50 – "Throwing his cloak aside, he jumped to his feet and came to Jesus."*

Lesson: Bartimaeus threw off his cloak, likely his only possession and source of security. He left behind his old life to receive what Jesus had for him.

Reflection: Is there something you need to let go of to fully follow Jesus—fear, security, sin, or comfort?

Challenge: Identify one thing you need to leave behind and surrender it to Jesus today. Trust Him for your future.

Day 5: Following Jesus in Gratitude

Scripture: *Mark 10:52 – "'Go,' said Jesus, 'your faith has healed you.' Immediately he received his sight and followed Jesus along the road."*

Lesson: After receiving his sight, Bartimaeus didn't go back to his old life. He followed Jesus in gratitude and commitment. True faith leads to discipleship.

Reflection: Are you following Jesus out of gratitude for what He's done in your life, or are you just seeking blessings?

Challenge: Take time today to thank Jesus for His goodness. Commit to following Him, not just for what He gives but for who He is.

Final Summary: What Bartimaeus Teaches Us

- **Day 1:** Recognize Jesus as the Messiah—He is your Savior and Lord.
- **Day 2:** Be persistent in faith—don't let opposition discourage you.
- **Day 3:** Ask boldly—believe in Jesus' power to do the impossible.
- **Day 4:** Leave behind the old life—follow Jesus without hesitation.
- **Day 5:** Follow Jesus in gratitude—live as a committed disciple.

Life Application: Which lesson inspired you the most? How will you let it affect your choices moving forward? Pray for a heart like Bartimaeus—persistent, bold, and full of gratitude as you follow Jesus.

Chapter 63

The Rich Young Ruler: Desire, Decision, and the Cost of Discipleship

(Matthew 19; Mark 10; Luke 18)

Day 1: Desiring Eternal Life

Scripture: *Mark 10:17 – "As Jesus started on His way, a man ran up to Him and fell on his knees before Him. 'Good teacher,' he asked, 'what must I do to inherit eternal life?'"*

Lesson: The rich young ruler genuinely desired eternal life. He approached Jesus with respect and sincerity, showing his spiritual hunger.

Reflection: Do you truly desire eternal life and a relationship with Jesus, or are you more focused on earthly pursuits?

Challenge: Reflect on your priorities today. Spend intentional time in prayer, expressing your desire to grow closer to Jesus.

Day 2: Keeping the Law but Lacking Relationship

Scripture: *Mark 10:19-20 – "'You know the commandments…'… 'Teacher,' he declared, 'all these I have kept since I was a boy.'"*

Lesson: The young man followed the commandments and was morally upright, but he lacked a personal relationship with Jesus. Obedience without love and surrender is incomplete.

Reflection: Are you focused on religious rules without pursuing a genuine relationship with Christ?

Challenge: Move beyond ritual to relationship. Talk to Jesus today as your friend and Savior, not just as a rule-giver.

Day 3: Facing the Cost of Discipleship

Scripture: *Mark 10:21 – "Jesus looked at him and loved him. 'One thing you lack,' He said. 'Go, sell everything you have and give to the poor, and you will have treasure in heaven. Then come, follow Me.'"*

Lesson: Jesus asked the young man to give up his wealth, not because wealth is evil, but because it was his greatest attachment. True discipleship requires surrendering whatever competes with Christ for your heart.

Reflection: What is competing for your heart? Is there something you're unwilling to give up for Jesus?

Challenge: Identify one thing you're holding onto tightly (money, status, security, or a relationship). Offer it to Jesus today, trusting Him with your future. If He asks you to walk away from it to follow Him, step out in faith and do it.

Day 4: Walking Away with a Heavy Heart

Scripture: *Mark 10:22 – "At this the man's face fell. He went away sad, because he had great wealth."*

Lesson: The young man couldn't let go of his wealth and walked away from Jesus. His attachment to earthly possessions outweighed his desire for eternal life.

Reflection: Are you holding onto something that is causing you to walk away from fully following Jesus?

Challenge: Choose Jesus over anything that's holding you back. Take a step of obedience today, even if it's difficult.

Day 5: The Reward of Surrender

Scripture: *Mark 10:29-30 – "'Truly I tell you,' Jesus replied, 'no one who has left home or brothers or sisters or mother or father or children or fields for Me and the Gospel will fail to receive a hundred times as much in this present age... and in the age to come eternal life.'"*

Lesson: Jesus promises that whatever we give up for Him will be repaid with far greater blessings, both now and eternally. Surrender leads to reward.

Reflection: Do you trust Jesus' promise that surrendering to Him leads to greater joy and fulfillment?

Challenge: Trust Jesus with your sacrifices. Write down one area of surrender and pray, believing in His promise to provide and bless you abundantly.

Final Summary: What The Rich Young Ruler Teaches Us

- **Day 1:** Desire Jesus above all—seek a relationship, not just blessings.
- **Day 2:** Pursue relationship, not just rules—love Jesus genuinely.
- **Day 3:** Count the cost of discipleship—be willing to surrender all.
- **Day 4:** Don't walk away from Jesus—choose Him over worldly attachments.
- **Day 5:** Trust in Jesus' reward—He repays what you surrender a hundredfold.

Life Application: Which lesson resonated with you the most? How will you continue to carry it out in your life? Pray for a heart willing to surrender all to Jesus, trusting in His goodness and promises.

Chapter 64

James (the Brother of Jesus): A Life of Wisdom, Humility, and Faith in Action

(Matthew 13; Mark 6; John 7; Acts 15,21; James)

Day 1: Growing in Humility and Faith

Scripture: *John 7:5 – "For even His own brothers did not believe in Him."*

Lesson: James didn't initially believe in Jesus as the Messiah, but later became a key leader in the early church. His transformation shows how God can change even the most skeptical hearts.

Reflection: Are there areas in your life where you struggle to fully trust Jesus?

Challenge: If you have doubts, bring them to God today. Ask Him to strengthen your faith and deepen your understanding of who Jesus is.

Day 2: Faith That Produces Action

Scripture: *James 2:17 – "In the same way, faith by itself, if it is not accompanied by action, is dead."*

Lesson: James emphasized that true faith is not just believing in God—it must be expressed through love, service, and obedience.

Reflection: Is your faith producing good works, or is it mostly just words?

Challenge: Find a way today to put your faith into action—serve someone in need, encourage a friend, or take a bold step of obedience.

Day 3: Controlling Your Tongue

Scripture: *James 3:5-6* – *"...the tongue is a small part of the body, but it makes great boasts... The tongue also is a fire, a world of evil among the parts of the body. It corrupts the whole body, sets the whole course of one's life on fire, and is itself set on fire by hell."*

Lesson: James warned that our words have great power. They can bring life or destruction, so we must be careful about how we speak.

Reflection: Are your words building others up, or do they cause harm and destruction?

Challenge: Be intentional about your words today. Speak life, encouragement, and truth instead of criticism, negativity, or vulgar joking.

Day 4: Submitting to God's Will

Scripture: *James 4:7* – *"Submit yourselves, then, to God. Resist the devil, and he will flee from you."*

Lesson: James taught that true wisdom comes from surrendering to God's authority. When we humble ourselves before Him, we gain strength to resist temptation.

Reflection: Are you fully submitting to God, or are you holding onto control in certain areas of your life?

Challenge: Surrender one area of your life to God today—whether a habit, decision, or struggle. Trust Him completely, and resist the temptation to return to doing things your own way.

Day 5: Persevering Through Trials

Scripture: *James 1:2-3* – *"Consider it pure joy, my brothers and sisters, whenever you face trials of many kinds, because you know that the testing of your faith produces perseverance."*

Lesson: James encouraged believers to see trials as opportunities to grow in faith. Challenges refine us and make us stronger in Christ.

Reflection: Are you viewing your struggles as a chance to grow, or are you letting them shake your faith?

Challenge: Choose to thank God today for a trial you're facing. Ask Him to use it to strengthen your character and faith.

Final Summary: What James Teaches Us

- **Day 1:** Faith grows—allow God to transform your heart.

- **Day 2:** Faith without action is dead—live out what you believe.

- **Day 3:** Your words matter—use them wisely.

- **Day 4:** Submit to God—resist temptation through obedience.

- **Day 5:** Trials refine you—embrace them as opportunities for growth.

Life Application: Which lesson challenged you the most? How will you put it into practice in your life? Pray for wisdom and strength to live a life of faith, humility, and perseverance like James.

Chapter 65

Pontius Pilate: Moral Weakness, Indecision, and Missed Truth

(Matthew 27-28; Mark 15; Luke 3,13,20,23; John 18-19)

Day 1: Facing the Truth but Avoiding Commitment

Scripture: *John 18:37-38 – "'You are a king, then!' said Pilate. Jesus answered, 'You say that I am a king. In fact, the reason I was born and came into the world is to testify to the truth. Everyone on the side of truth listens to me.' 'What is truth?' retorted Pilate. With this he went out again to the Jews gathered there and said, 'I find no basis for a charge against him.'"*

Lesson: Pilate stood face-to-face with Jesus, the source of all truth, yet he dismissed the conversation without seeking real understanding. His question, *"What is truth?"*, reveals his uncertainty and unwillingness to commit.

Reflection: Are you fully embracing the truth of Christ, or are you avoiding deep commitment out of fear or uncertainty?

Challenge: Take time today to reflect on an area where you have been hesitant to fully embrace God's truth. Ask Him to give you courage to walk in full obedience and faith.

Day 2: Pleasing People Instead of Doing What Is Right

Scripture: *Matthew 27:22-24 – "'What shall I do, then, with Jesus who is called the Messiah?' Pilate asked. They all answered, 'Crucify him!' 'Why? What crime has he* *committed?' asked Pilate. But they shouted all the louder, 'Crucify him!' When Pilate saw that he was getting nowhere, but that instead an uproar was starting, he took water and washed his hands in front of the crowd. 'I am innocent of this man's blood,' he said. 'It is your responsibility!'"*

Lesson: Pilate knew Jesus was innocent, yet he caved under pressure from the crowd. Instead of standing for justice, he sought to avoid responsibility.

Reflection: Are you making decisions based on what is right, or are you allowing the fear of others' opinions to control you?

Challenge: Commit today to stand for truth, even if it is unpopular. Ask God for the courage to do what is right instead of what is easy.

Day 3: Trying to Shift Responsibility for Our Choices

Scripture: *Matthew 27:24 – "...he took water and washed his hands in front of the crowd. 'I am innocent of this man's blood,' he said. 'It is your responsibility!'"*

Lesson: Pilate thought he could remove guilt by washing his hands, but responsibility doesn't disappear through avoidance. We are accountable for our choices.

Reflection: Are there areas in your life where you are avoiding responsibility instead of facing it?

Challenge: If you've been trying to avoid responsibility for a decision or action, take ownership today. Ask God for wisdom and strength to do what is right. If you need to, repent for a situation where you have participated in sin or injustice by not taking responsibility for your role in the situation.

Day 4: Ignoring Warnings from God

Scripture: *Matthew 27:19 – "While Pilate was sitting on the judge's seat, his wife sent him this message: 'Don't have anything to do with that innocent man, for I have suffered a great deal today in a dream because of him.'"*

Lesson: God sent Pilate a warning through his wife, yet he ignored it. Sometimes, God speaks to us through people, but we choose not to listen.

Reflection: Are you ignoring any warnings from God, whether through Scripture, wise counsel, or conviction in your heart?

Challenge: Pay attention today to how God might be speaking to you. If He has been warning you about something, respond with obedience rather than avoidance.

Day 5: Failing to Recognize the Savior

Scripture: *John 19:10-11 – "'Do you refuse to speak to me?' Pilate said. 'Don't you realize I have power either to free you or to crucify you?' Jesus answered, 'You would have no power over me if it were not given to you from above...'"*

Lesson: Pilate thought he had control over Jesus' fate, but Jesus reminded him that all authority comes from God. Pilate missed the opportunity to recognize and respond to the true King.

Reflection: Are you trying to control your life instead of surrendering to Jesus' authority?

Challenge: Surrender an area of your life where you have been trying to take control. Acknowledge that Jesus is Lord over all.

Final Summary: What Pontius Pilate Teaches Us

- **Day 1:** Don't ignore the truth—seek and embrace Christ fully.
- **Day 2:** Do what is right, not what pleases people.
- **Day 3:** Take responsibility for your choices—don't shift blame.
- **Day 4:** Listen to God's warnings—He speaks through Scripture, people, and conviction.
- **Day 5:** Surrender control—recognize Jesus as Lord over your life.

Life Application: Which lesson convicted you the most? How will you apply it in your life going forward? Pray for the courage to seek truth, stand firm in righteousness, and fully surrender to Jesus.

Chapter 66

Jude: Contending for the Faith, Warning Against Deception, and Trusting in God's Power

(Jude)

Day 1: Contending for the Faith

Scripture: *Jude 1:3* – *"Dear friends, although I was very eager to write to you about the salvation we share, I felt compelled to write and urge you to contend for the faith that was once for all entrusted to God's holy people."*

Lesson: Jude originally intended to write about salvation but was led by the Spirit to urge believers to fight for the truth of the Gospel. He knew faith must be actively defended.

Reflection: Are you standing firm in your faith, or do you hesitate when faced with opposition?

Challenge: Be bold in defending biblical truth today. Speak up when you see compromise, and encourage others to stay strong in their faith.

Day 2: Recognizing False Teachers

Scripture: *Jude 1:4* – *"For certain individuals whose condemnation was written about long ago have secretly slipped in among you. They are ungodly people, who pervert the grace of our God into a license for immorality..."*

Lesson: Jude warned against false teachers who distort God's grace. We must be discerning and compare everything to Scripture.

Reflection: Are you careful about the teachings you follow? Do you test everything against God's Word?

Challenge: Examine the content you consume—whether books, sermons, music, shows, or online messages. Make sure they align with Scripture.

Day 3: Learning from Past Warnings

Scripture: *Jude 1:5 – "Though you already know all this, I want to remind you that the Lord at one time delivered His people out of Egypt, but later destroyed those who did not believe."*

Lesson: Jude reminded believers that throughout history, rebellion against God led to destruction. He urged them to learn from the past.

Reflection: Are you learning from past mistakes—both your own and those recorded in Scripture?

Challenge: Take time today to reflect on past lessons God has taught you. Ask Him to help you stay on the right path.

Day 4: Keeping Yourself in God's Love

Scripture: *Jude 1:20-21 – "But you, dear friends, by building yourselves up in your most holy faith and praying in the Holy Spirit, keep yourselves in God's love..."*

Lesson: Jude gave practical advice for staying strong in faith—build yourself up through Scripture, prayer, and a close, loving relationship with God.

Reflection: Are you actively growing in your faith, or are you becoming spiritually complacent?

Challenge: Strengthen your faith today by spending intentional time in Scripture and prayer.

Day 5: Trusting God to Keep You Strong

Scripture: *Jude 1:24 – "To him who is able to keep you from stumbling and to present you before his glorious presence without fault and with great joy."*

Lesson: Ultimately, it is God who sustains us. We must rely on Him, knowing He is able to keep us from falling and will bring us into His presence with joy.

Reflection: Are you trusting in your own strength, or are you looking to God to sustain your faith?

Challenge: Surrender any struggles to God today. Trust Him to keep you strong and faithful in your walk with Him.

Final Summary: What Jude Teaches Us

- **Day 1:** Contend for the faith—stand firm in biblical truth.
- **Day 2:** Be discerning—watch out for false teaching.
- **Day 3:** Learn from past mistakes—stay faithful to God.
- **Day 4:** Grow spiritually—build yourself up in prayer and Scripture.
- **Day 5:** Trust God to sustain you—He will keep you strong.

Life Application: Which lesson struck you the most? How will you incorporate it in your life going forward? Pray for wisdom, discernment, and strength as you stand firm in your faith and trust God to guide you.

Chapter 67

Stephen: A Life of Boldness, Wisdom, and Faithfulness Unto Death

(Acts 6-8)

Day 1: A Man Full of Faith and the Holy Spirit

Scripture: *Acts 6:5 – "...They chose Stephen, a man full of faith and of the Holy Spirit..."*

Lesson: Stephen wasn't just chosen because he was capable—he was chosen because he was full of faith and filled with the Holy Spirit. His spiritual life was his greatest qualification.

Reflection: Are you relying on your own abilities, or are you allowing God's Spirit to fill and guide you?

Challenge: Pray today for a fresh filling of the Holy Spirit. Ask God to strengthen your faith and lead you in everything you do.

Day 2: Serving Faithfully in Small Things

Scripture: *Acts 6:1-3,5,8 – "...their widows were being overlooked in the daily distribution of food. So the Twelve... said, "...Brothers and sisters, choose seven men from among you who are known to be full of the Spirit and wisdom. We will turn this responsibility over to them... They chose Stephen...Now Stephen, a man full of God's grace and power, performed great wonders and signs among the people."*

Lesson: Stephen was originally chosen to help distribute food to widows, yet he served with excellence. His faithfulness in small things led to greater opportunities.

Reflection: Are you being faithful in the small tasks God has given you, or are you waiting for something "bigger" before you serve wholeheartedly?

Challenge: Whatever task you have today, do it with excellence as if serving the Lord.

Day 3: Boldly Speaking the Truth

Scripture: *Acts 7:51 – "You stiff-necked people! Your hearts and ears are still uncircumcised. You are just like your ancestors: You always resist the Holy Spirit!"*

Lesson: Stephen didn't hold back in preaching the truth, even when it was unpopular. He spoke boldly, knowing it could cost him everything.

Reflection: Are you afraid to speak the truth because of what others might think?

Challenge: Share a biblical truth with someone today—whether in a conversation, social media, or encouragement to a friend. Speak with boldness and love.

Day 4: Keeping Your Eyes on Jesus in Trials

Scripture: *Acts 7:55 – "But Stephen, full of the Holy Spirit, looked up to heaven and saw the glory of God, and Jesus standing at the right hand of God."*

Lesson: Even as he was being stoned to death, Stephen's focus remained on Jesus. His trials did not shake his faith or distract him from his eternal hope.

Reflection: When you face challenges, do you focus on Jesus, or do you let fear and pain control your response?

Challenge: If you're struggling with a trial today, take a moment to shift your focus to Jesus. Worship, pray, or meditate on His promises.

Day 5: Forgiving Like Jesus

Scripture: *Acts 7:60 – "Then he fell on his knees and cried out, 'Lord, do not hold this sin against them.' When he had said this, he fell asleep."*

Lesson: Just like Jesus on the cross, Stephen forgave those who were killing him. His love and mercy reflected Christ even in his final moments.

Reflection: Is there someone in your life you need to forgive? Are you holding onto bitterness instead of showing grace?

Challenge: Choose to forgive someone today, even if they haven't apologized. Pray for them and release any resentment in your heart. Reflect on Jesus' forgiveness, freely given to you.

Final Summary: What Stephen Teaches Us

- **Day 1:** Seek to be full of faith and the Holy Spirit.
- **Day 2:** Serve faithfully—even in small things.
- **Day 3:** Speak the truth boldly—no matter the cost.
- **Day 4:** Keep your eyes on Jesus in trials.
- **Day 5:** Forgive like Jesus, even when it's difficult.

Life Application: Which lesson spoke to you the most? How will you continue to live it out? Pray for the boldness, faith, and grace to live as Stephen did—fully devoted to Christ until the very end.

Chapter 68

Philip the Evangelist: Bold Proclamation, Obedience to the Spirit, and Transforming Lives

(Acts 6,8,21)

Day 1: Preaching Christ Boldly in Difficult Places

Scripture: *Acts 8:5 – "Philip went down to a city in Samaria and proclaimed the Messiah there."*

Lesson: After persecution scattered the believers, Philip went to Samaria—a place avoided by many Jews—to boldly preach Christ. He didn't let cultural prejudices or fear stop him.

Reflection: Are you willing to share Jesus boldly, even in places or with people who might seem "difficult" or different from you?

Challenge: Step out of your comfort zone today and share the Gospel with someone you wouldn't normally approach.

Day 2: Demonstrating the Power of the Gospel

Scripture: *Acts 8:6-7 – "When the crowds heard Philip and saw the signs he performed, they all paid close attention to what he said. For with shrieks, impure spirits came out of many, and many who were paralyzed or lame were healed."*

Lesson: Philip's ministry wasn't just words—it was accompanied by miracles and deliverance. His life demonstrated the power of the Gospel.

Reflection: Are you living in a way that demonstrates the power and love of Jesus, or are your words empty?

Challenge: Pray boldly today for God's power to work through you. Be willing to pray for healing, deliverance, or any need someone has.

Day 3: Obedience to the Holy Spirit's Prompting

Scripture: *Acts 8:26-27 – "Now an angel of the Lord said to Philip, 'Go south to the road—the desert road—that goes down from Jerusalem to Gaza.' So he started out, and on his way he met an Ethiopian eunuch..."*

Lesson: Philip obeyed God's instruction without question, even though it meant going to a deserted place. His obedience led to a divine appointment that changed a nation.

Reflection: Are you sensitive to the Holy Spirit's prompting, even when it doesn't make sense?

Challenge: Listen for the Holy Spirit's leading today (and every day). Obey immediately, even if it seems inconvenient or unusual.

Day 4: Explaining Scripture and Leading Others to Christ

Scripture: *Acts 8:30, 35 – "Then Philip ran up to the chariot and heard the man reading Isaiah the prophet. 'Do you understand what you are reading?' Philip asked... Then Philip began with that very passage of Scripture and told him the good news about Jesus."*

Lesson: Philip met the Ethiopian eunuch where he was, explained the Scriptures, and pointed him to Jesus. He showed that effective evangelism involves listening, understanding, and guiding people to Christ.

Reflection: Are you equipped to explain the Gospel clearly, meeting people where they are in their understanding?

Challenge: Study a key passage of Scripture today that explains the Gospel. Be prepared to share it when the opportunity arises, and pray that God would give you that opportunity.

Day 5: Discipling and Leading to Baptism

Scripture: *Acts 8:36-38 – "As they traveled along the road, they came to some water and the eunuch said, 'Look, here is water. What can stand in the way of my being baptized?'... Then both Philip and the eunuch went down into the water and Philip baptized him."*

Lesson: Philip didn't just share the Gospel; he guided the eunuch to the next step—baptism. He understood the importance of discipleship and commitment.

Reflection: Are you helping others take the next step in their faith journey, or are you just sharing the basics of the Gospel?

Challenge: If you know someone who is exploring faith, encourage them to take the next step—whether it's baptism, joining a Bible study, or another act of commitment.

Final Summary: What Philip the Evangelist Teaches Us

- **Day 1:** Boldly preach Christ—even in difficult places.
- **Day 2:** Demonstrate the power of the Gospel—let your actions speak.
- **Day 3:** Obey the Holy Spirit—follow His leading without hesitation.
- **Day 4:** Explain the Gospel clearly—meet people where they are.
- **Day 5:** Lead others to commitment—guide them to the next step in faith.

Life Application: Which lesson challenged you the most? How will you let it affect your decisions going forward? Pray for a heart like Philip the Evangelist—bold, obedient, and effective in leading others to Christ.

Chapter 69

The Ethiopian Eunuch: Seeking Truth, Divine Appointment, and Joyful Conversion

(Acts 8)

Day 1: A Heart Seeking Truth

Scripture: *Acts 8:27-28 – "…an Ethiopian eunuch, an important official in charge of all the treasury of the Kandake (which means 'queen of the Ethiopians'). This man had gone to Jerusalem to worship, and on his way home was sitting in his chariot reading the Book of Isaiah the prophet."*

Lesson: The Ethiopian Eunuch was a man of influence and wealth, yet he was seeking spiritual truth. His journey to Jerusalem and his study of Scripture showed his genuine hunger for God.

Reflection: Are you actively seeking truth and a deeper understanding of God's Word, or are you spiritually complacent?

Challenge: Dedicate extra time today to study God's Word. Approach it with a heart hungry for truth and a desire to grow closer to God.

Day 2: Divine Appointment and Guidance

Scripture: *Acts 8:29-30 – "The Spirit told Philip, 'Go to that chariot and stay near it.' Then Philip ran up to the chariot and heard the man reading Isaiah the prophet. 'Do you understand what you are reading?' Philip asked."*

Lesson: God orchestrated a divine encounter between Philip and the Ethiopian. When we seek truth, God faithfully sends guidance and understanding.

Reflection: Are you open to the people and opportunities God places in your path to guide you in truth?

Challenge: Be attentive today for divine appointments—whether through a conversation, sermon, or reading. Seek God's guidance and be willing to learn.

Day 3: Humility and Willingness to Learn

Scripture: *Acts 8:31 – "'How can I,' he said, 'unless someone explains it to me?' So he invited Philip to come up and sit with him."*

Lesson: Despite his status and wealth, the Ethiopian Eunuch was humble enough to admit his need for understanding, even to a stranger on the side of the road. True wisdom comes from a teachable heart.

Reflection: Are you willing to learn from others, regardless of their status, age, or background?

Challenge: Seek wisdom from someone today—whether by asking a question about a spiritual topic you have been contemplating, reading a book, or listening to a teaching. Approach it with a humble heart.

Day 4: Understanding and Accepting the Gospel

Scripture: *Acts 8:34-35 – "The eunuch asked Philip, 'Tell me, please, who is the prophet talking about, himself or someone else?' Then Philip began with that very passage of Scripture and told him the good news about Jesus."*

Lesson: Philip explained how the prophecy in Isaiah pointed to Jesus. The Ethiopian Eunuch's questions led to his understanding of the Gospel, showing that seeking leads to finding.

Reflection: Do you tend to skip over things you do not understand? Are you asking the right questions and seeking to understand the full truth of the Gospel?

Challenge: Reflect on any questions you have about your faith. Seek answers today through prayer, Scripture, or a trusted spiritual mentor.

Day 5: Joyful Obedience and Baptism

Scripture: *Acts 8:36, 39 – "As they traveled along the road, they came to some water and the eunuch said, 'Look, here is water. What can stand in the way of my being baptized?'... When they came up out of the water, the Spirit of the LORD suddenly took Philip away, and the eunuch did not see him again, but went on his way rejoicing."*

Lesson: The Ethiopian Eunuch responded to the Gospel with immediate obedience, getting baptized without hesitation. His joy was a result of his newfound salvation.

Reflection: Are you quick to obey God's Word, or do you hesitate and make excuses? What have you been procrastinating?

Challenge: Choose to obey God in one area today without delay. Let your obedience be joyful, knowing it brings you closer to Him.

Final Summary: What The Ethiopian Eunuch Teaches Us

- **Day 1:** Seek truth—approach God's Word with hunger and desire for understanding.
- **Day 2:** Be open to divine appointments—God sends guidance when you seek Him.
- **Day 3:** Stay teachable—humility leads to wisdom.
- **Day 4:** Ask the right questions—seeking leads to finding the truth.
- **Day 5:** Obey joyfully—immediate obedience brings joy and growth.

Life Application: Which lesson stood out to you the most? How will you continue to carry it out? Pray for a heart like the Ethiopian Eunuch—hungry for truth, humble to learn, and joyful in obedience.

Chapter 70

Cornelius: A Life of Devotion, Obedience, and God's Inclusive Grace

(Acts 10-11)

Day 1: A Devoted and God-Fearing Man

Scripture: *Acts 10:2 – "He and all his family were devout and God-fearing; he gave generously to those in need and prayed to God regularly."*

Lesson: Cornelius was a Roman centurion, yet he was devoted to God even before knowing Christ. His faith was reflected in his generosity and prayer life.

Reflection: Is your life marked by devotion, generosity, and prayer?

Challenge: Spend extra time in prayer today and look for a way to be generous to someone in need.

Day 2: God Sees and Hears You

Scripture: *Acts 10:4 – "Cornelius stared at him in fear. 'What is it, Lord?' he asked. The angel answered, 'Your prayers and gifts to the poor have come up as a memorial offering before God.'"*

Lesson: God took notice of Cornelius' faithfulness. His prayers and generosity were seen and valued by God, and God showed up to Cornelius in a very personal way.

Reflection: Do you believe that God sees and values your faithfulness, even in small things? Is there an area in which you could improve concerning faithfulness?

Challenge: Trust that your obedience and prayers matter. Take time today to thank God for always seeing and hearing you. If there is an area where you have struggled to be faithful—even in a small thing—confess it, repent, and take at least one small step of obedience in that area.

Day 3: Obedience Without Hesitation

Scripture: *Acts 10:7-8 – "When the angel who spoke to him had gone, Cornelius called two of his servants and a devout soldier... He told them everything that had happened and sent them to Joppa."*

Lesson: Cornelius didn't delay in obeying God's command. He sent for Peter immediately, showing his willingness to follow God's leading.

Reflection: Do you obey God immediately, or do you hesitate?

Challenge: Act in obedience today. If God has put something on your heart—whether it's helping someone, forgiving, or sharing the Gospel—do it without delay.

Day 4: God's Grace is for All People

Scripture: *Acts 10:34-35 – "Then Peter began to speak: 'I now realize how true it is that God does not show favoritism but accepts from every nation the one who fears Him and does what is right.'"*

Lesson: Cornelius' story marked a turning point in Peter's understanding of God's grace—the Gospel was not just for the Jews but for all people. God welcomes anyone who seeks Him.

Reflection: Do you sometimes limit God's grace to certain types of people? Are you open to sharing Christ with everyone, regardless of background?

Challenge: Reach out to someone today who is different from you. Show God's love and inclusiveness in your words and actions.

Day 5: A Household Transformed

Scripture: *Acts 10:44 – "While Peter was still speaking these words, the Holy Spirit came on all who heard the message."*

Lesson: Because of Cornelius' faith and obedience, his entire household experienced salvation and the power of the Holy Spirit.

Reflection: Is your faith impacting those around you? Are you leading your family, friends, and community closer to Christ?

Challenge: Pray today for your household or someone close to you. Ask God to work in their lives through your example and testimony. Be open to God creating an opportunity for you to actively encourage them toward greater faith today.

Final Summary: What Cornelius Teaches Us

- **Day 1:** Live a life of devotion—pray and give generously.
- **Day 2:** Trust that God sees and hears you.
- **Day 3:** Obey immediately when God calls.
- **Day 4:** Recognize that God's grace is for all people.
- **Day 5:** Let your faith transform those around you.

Life Application: Which lesson resonated with you the most? How will you continue to practice it moving forward? Pray for a heart like Cornelius—devoted, obedient, and open to God's greater plan.

Chapter 71

Paul: A Life of Transformation, Boldness, and Endurance

(Acts 9,11-28; Romans; I and II Corinthians; Galatians; Ephesians; Philippians; Colossians; I and II Thessalonians; I and II Timothy; Titus; Philemon)

Day 1: God Can Transform Anyone

Scripture: *Acts 9:15 – "But the Lord said to Ananias, 'Go! This man is my chosen instrument to proclaim my name to the Gentiles and their kings and to the people of Israel.'"*

Lesson: Paul (formerly Saul) was a persecutor of Christians, "breathing out murderous threats against them" (Acts 9:1), before God transformed his life by blinding him in the middle of the road and sending Ananias to share the Gospel with him and pray for his healing. Paul's story is proof that no one is beyond God's reach.

Reflection: Do you believe that God can transform even the most unlikely people—including you?

Challenge: Pray for someone who seems impossibly far from God. Ask Him to work in their life as He did in Paul's.

Day 2: Living by Faith, Not by Sight

Scripture: *2 Corinthians 5:7 – "For we live by faith, not by sight."*

Lesson: Once Paul became a believer and stepped into his calling as an Apostle, he endured hardships, imprisonments, and persecution, yet he never lost sight of his faith. He trusted in what he could not see.

Reflection: Are you walking by faith, or do you rely only on what is visible and logical?

Challenge: Take one step today that requires faith—whether in your career, relationships, or spiritual life. Trust that God is leading you.

Day 3: Finding Strength in Weakness

Scripture: *2 Corinthians 12:9 – "But He said to me, 'My grace is sufficient for you, for my power is made perfect in weakness.'"*

Lesson: Paul struggled with a "thorn in the flesh," but instead of removing it, God used it to keep Paul humble and dependent on Him.

Reflection: Do you see your weaknesses as obstacles, or as opportunities for God's strength to shine?

Challenge: Surrender your weaknesses to God today. Let Him use them for His glory instead of trying to rely on your own strength.

Day 4: Pressing On Toward the Goal

Scripture: *Philippians 3:13-14 – "...Forgetting what is behind and straining toward what is ahead, I press on toward the goal to win the prize for which God has called me heavenward in Christ Jesus."*

Lesson: Paul didn't let his past failures define him. He focused on his mission and kept moving forward in faith.

Reflection: Are you holding onto past mistakes, or are you pressing forward in God's calling?

Challenge: Let go of something from your past that is holding you back. Step forward in faith toward the future God has for you.

Day 5: Finishing the Race Well

Scripture: *2 Timothy 4:7 – "I have fought the good fight, I have finished the race, I have kept the faith."*

Lesson: Paul endured until the very end, remaining faithful despite suffering. His life was fully poured out for the Gospel.

Reflection: Are you living in a way that will allow you to finish well in your faith?

Challenge: Commit to one spiritual discipline today (prayer, Bible study, worship) that will help you stay faithful and finish strong.

Final Summary: What Paul Teaches Us

- **Day 1:** No one is beyond God's transformation—He can use anyone.
- **Day 2:** Live by faith—trust God beyond what you can see.
- **Day 3:** Embrace weakness—God's power is strongest when we rely on Him.
- **Day 4:** Let go of the past—keep pressing toward God's calling.
- **Day 5:** Stay faithful to the end—live with eternity in mind.

Life Application: Which lesson do you need to practice the most? How will you do that moving forward? Pray for the strength to live boldly for Christ, endure hardships with faith, and finish the race well.

Chapter 72

Ananias (Who Prayed for Saul/Paul): Obedience, Courage, and Spiritual Restoration

(Acts 9)

Day 1: Hearing God's Voice and Responding

Scripture: *Acts 9:10 – "In Damascus there was a disciple named Ananias. The Lord called to him in a vision, 'Ananias!' 'Yes, Lord,' he answered."*

Lesson: Ananias was attentive to God's voice and responded immediately. He was sensitive to the Holy Spirit's leading and ready to listen.

Reflection: Are you listening for God's voice, or are you too busy or distracted?

Challenge: Take time today to quiet your mind and listen for God's guidance. Be open to His leading, even if it challenges your comfort zone.

Day 2: Obeying Even When It's Hard

Scripture: *Acts 9:11 – "The Lord told him, 'Go to the house of Judas on Straight Street and ask for a man from Tarsus named Saul, for he is praying.'"*

Lesson: Ananias was called to help Saul, who was known for persecuting Christians. Obeying God meant risking his safety and trusting God's purpose.

Reflection: Are you willing to obey God's call, even when it feels risky or uncomfortable?

Challenge: Take a step of faith today in obedience to God, even if it challenges your comfort or security. Trust in His protection and purpose.

Day 3: Overcoming Fear with Faith

Scripture: *Acts 9:13-14 – "'Lord,' Ananias answered, 'I have heard many reports about this man and all the harm he has done to Your holy people in Jerusalem. And he has come here with authority from the chief priests to arrest all who call on Your name.'"*

Lesson: Ananias was honest with God about his fears, but he didn't let fear stop him from obeying. He trusted God's word over his own understanding.

Reflection: Are you allowing fear to stop you from stepping into God's calling?

Challenge: Identify one fear that's holding you back. Confront it with faith, trusting in God's promise to be with you.

Day 4: Being an Instrument of Healing and Restoration

Scripture: *Acts 9:17 – "Then Ananias went to the house and entered it. Placing his hands on Saul, he said, 'Brother Saul, the Lord—Jesus, who appeared to you on the road as you were coming here—has sent me so that you may see again and be filled with the Holy Spirit.'"*

Lesson: Ananias was willing to be God's instrument of healing and restoration. He laid hands on Saul, calling him "Brother," showing forgiveness and acceptance despite all the hurt Saul had caused to so many believers.

Reflection: Are you willing to be an agent of healing, forgiveness, and restoration in someone's life?

Challenge: Reach out today to someone who needs encouragement, forgiveness, or restoration. Following the leading of the Holy Spirit, be God's instrument of grace and healing.

Day 5: Obedience Leads to Transformation

Scripture: *Acts 9:18-19 – "Immediately, something like scales fell from Saul's eyes, and he could see again. He got up and was baptized, and after taking some food, he regained his strength."*

Lesson: Because of Ananias' obedience, Saul (later known as Paul) was healed, baptized, and filled with the Holy Spirit. Ananias' faithfulness played a role in the transformation of one of the greatest apostles.

Reflection: Are you willing to obey God, knowing your obedience could impact someone else's destiny?

Challenge: Take one step of obedience today, no matter how small, trusting that God can use it to bring transformation in someone's life.

Final Summary: What Ananias Teaches Us

- **Day 1:** Listen for God's voice—be attentive and willing to respond.

- **Day 2:** Obey God even when it's hard—step out in faith.

- **Day 3:** Confront fear with faith—trust in God's protection and purpose.

- **Day 4:** Be an instrument of healing—bring grace and restoration to others.

- **Day 5:** Trust in the power of obedience—God uses it for transformation.

Life Application: Which lesson convicted you the most? How will you continue to apply it going forward? Pray for a heart like Ananias—obedient, courageous, and willing to be used by God for His purposes.

Chapter 73

Barnabas: A Life of Encouragement, Generosity, and Faithfulness

(Acts 4, 9, 11-15)

Day 1: Encouraging Others in Their Faith

Scripture: *Acts 11:23-24 – "When he arrived and saw what the grace of God had done, he was glad and encouraged them all to remain true to the Lord with all their hearts. He was a good man, full of the Holy Spirit and faith, and a great number of people were brought to the Lord."*

Lesson: Barnabas was known as an encourager. His words and actions strengthened the faith of others and helped the early church grow.

Reflection: Are you an encourager to those around you? Do you build others up in their true identity and their walk with Christ?

Challenge: Encourage at least one person today—through a message, prayer, or kind words. Let them know how they are making a difference.

Day 2: Generosity as a Lifestyle

Scripture: *Acts 4:36-37 – "Joseph, a Levite from Cyprus, whom the apostles called Barnabas (which means 'son of encouragement'), sold a field he owned and brought the money and put it at the apostles' feet."*

Lesson: Barnabas didn't just encourage with words—he also gave generously to support God's work. His open-handed giving helped fuel the mission of the church.

Reflection: Are you using your resources—time, money, and talents—to bless others and further God's kingdom?

Challenge: Give sacrificially today. It could be financial support for a ministry, an act of service, or simply helping someone in need.

Day 3: Believing in People When Others Don't

Scripture: *Acts 9:26-27 – "When he (Saul) came to Jerusalem, he tried to join the disciples, but they were all afraid of him, not believing that he really was a disciple. But Barnabas took him and brought him to the apostles..."*

Lesson: While others doubted Paul's transformation, Barnabas believed in him and helped him gain acceptance. His trust changed the course of Paul's ministry.

Reflection: Do you judge people based on their past, or do you believe in God's ability to transform them?

Challenge: Show grace to someone today who may have a difficult past. Offer them encouragement and remind them that God can use anyone.

Day 4: Partnering in God's Work

Scripture: *Acts 13:2-3 – "While they were worshiping the Lord and fasting, the Holy Spirit said, 'Set apart for me Barnabas and Saul for the work to which I have called them.' So after they had fasted and prayed, they placed their hands on them and sent them off."*

Lesson: Barnabas partnered with Paul in missionary work, showing that ministry is best done together. He valued teamwork in advancing God's kingdom.

Reflection: Are you working alongside others in God's mission, or are you trying to serve alone?

Challenge: Find a way to support or partner with someone in ministry today—whether through prayer, service, or encouragement.

Day 5: Handling Disagreements with Grace

Scripture: *Acts 15:39-40 – "They had such a sharp disagreement that they parted company. Barnabas took Mark and sailed for Cyprus, but Paul chose Silas and left…"*

Lesson: Barnabas and Paul disagreed over John Mark, but Barnabas chose to support Mark despite past failures. Later, Mark became a key leader in the church.

Reflection: How do you handle disagreements? Do you extend grace and seek reconciliation, or do you hold onto division?

Challenge: If there's someone you've had a disagreement with, reach out today in grace. Seek peace and unity in your relationships.

Final Summary: What Barnabas Teaches Us

- **Day 1:** Be an encourager—help others stay strong in faith.
- **Day 2:** Live generously—use your resources to bless others.
- **Day 3:** Believe in people—trust in God's power to transform lives.
- **Day 4:** Work in partnership—God's mission is best done together.
- **Day 5:** Handle disagreements with grace—prioritize unity.

Life Application: Which lesson inspired you the most? How will you live it out going forward? Pray for a heart like Barnabas—full of encouragement, generosity, and grace.

Chapter 74

Mark (John Mark): Growth, Second Chances, and Faithfulness

(Acts 12-13,15; Colossians 4; II Timothy 4; Philemon; I Peter 5)

Day 1: A Humble Beginning

Scripture: *Acts 12:12* – *"When this had dawned on him, he went to the house of Mary, the mother of John, also called Mark, where many people had gathered and were praying."*

Lesson: John Mark grew up in a household of faith. His mother hosted early Christian gatherings, making him familiar with the work of the Gospel from a young age.

Reflection: Are you nurturing your faith and making space for God to work in your life?

Challenge: Dedicate time today to grow in your faith—whether by prayer, Bible reading, or listening to a sermon.

Day 2: Facing Failure and Disappointment

Scripture: *Acts 13:13* – *"...Paul and his companions sailed to Perga in Pamphylia, where John left them to return to Jerusalem."*

Lesson: John Mark abandoned Paul and Barnabas on their missionary journey. His early failure caused disappointment but wasn't the end of his story.

Reflection: Have you ever failed in your faith journey and felt disqualified? Remember that failure isn't final with God.

Challenge: If you've been discouraged by past mistakes, bring them to God today. Trust that He still has a plan for you.

Day 3: A Second Chance

Scripture: *2 Timothy 4:11 – "...Get Mark and bring him with you, because he is helpful to me in my ministry."*

Lesson: Though Paul once rejected John Mark for ministry (Acts 15:37-39), later he saw his growth and valued him as a partner in spreading the Gospel.

Reflection: Are you holding onto past failures instead of stepping into the second chances God offers?

Challenge: Ask God to restore you in any area where you feel unworthy. Take a step today to serve Him despite past setbacks.

Day 4: Serving Behind the Scenes

Scripture: *1 Peter 5:13 – "She who is in Babylon, chosen together with you, sends you her greetings, and so does my son Mark."*

Lesson: John Mark served alongside both Peter and Paul, supporting their ministry. He didn't seek the spotlight but was faithful behind the scenes.

Reflection: Are you content serving in ways that may not bring personal recognition?

Challenge: Find a way to serve quietly today—help someone in need, support your church, or encourage a friend without seeking attention.

Day 5: Leaving a Lasting Impact

Scripture: *Mark 1:1 – "The beginning of the good news about Jesus the Messiah, the Son of God."*

Lesson: Despite his failures, John Mark later wrote the Gospel of Mark, one of the most influential books of the Bible, preserving Jesus' story for future generations.

Reflection: Are you living in a way that leaves a lasting spiritual impact?

Challenge: Think of one way you can make a difference for God's kingdom—mentoring someone, sharing your testimony, or supporting a ministry. Take action today.

Final Summary: What Mark Teaches Us

- **Day 1:** Start where you are—nurture your faith.

- **Day 2:** Failure isn't final—God still has a purpose for you.

- **Day 3:** Accept second chances—God restores and redeems.

- **Day 4:** Serve humbly—faithfulness matters more than recognition.

- **Day 5:** Leave a spiritual legacy—live in a way that impacts future generations.

Life Application: Which lesson spoke to you the most? How will you continue to incorporate it in your life? Pray for the strength to persevere, serve faithfully, and trust in God's grace, just as Mark did.

Chapter 75

Luke: A Life of Precision, Compassion, and Dedication to the Gospel

(Luke 1; Acts 1; Colossians 4; II Timothy 4; Philemon)

Day 1: Using Your Gifts for God's Kingdom

Scripture: *Colossians 4:14 – "Our dear friend Luke, the doctor, and Demas send greetings."*

Lesson: Luke was a physician, but he used his skills to serve God's kingdom. Instead of seeking personal success, he dedicated his profession to advancing the Gospel.

Reflection: Are you using your talents and skills to glorify God?

Challenge: Find one way today to use your gifts—whether in your job, ministry, or everyday life—to serve God and others.

Day 2: Seeking Truth and Accuracy

Scripture: *Luke 1:3-4 – "With this in mind, since I myself have carefully investigated everything from the beginning, I too decided to write an orderly account for you... so that you may know the certainty of the things you have been taught."*

Lesson: Luke wasn't an eyewitness to Jesus' ministry, but he diligently investigated the truth. He valued accuracy, ensuring the Gospel message was clearly and faithfully recorded.

Reflection: Are you seeking truth in your faith journey, or are you relying on secondhand information?

Challenge: Spend extra time in Scripture today, seeking to deepen your understanding of God's Word.

Day 3: Compassion for the Marginalized

Scripture: *Luke 5:31-32 – "Jesus answered them, 'It is not the healthy who need a doctor, but the sick. I have not come to call the righteous, but sinners to repentance.'"*

Lesson: Luke's Gospel emphasizes Jesus' care for the outcasts—tax collectors, the poor, the sinful, and the sick. Like Jesus, Luke had a heart for the broken.

Reflection: Are you showing compassion to those society often ignores?

Challenge: Reach out today to someone who may feel overlooked or who is struggling. Show them kindness and Christ's love.

Day 4: Staying Faithful in Ministry

Scripture: *2 Timothy 4:11 – "Only Luke is with me..."*

Lesson: When Paul was imprisoned and abandoned by many, Luke remained by his side. His loyalty and faithfulness made him a trusted companion in the ministry.

Reflection: Are you committed to coming alongside and supporting those in your life who are struggling? Are you willing to walk alongside people even when they are dealing with painful or difficult circumstances?

Challenge: Ask God to show you someone in your life who is struggling and needs someone to come alongside them. Follow the Holy Spirit's leading, and find a way to let that person know that they are not alone. Be willing to stay present with them in the midst of their struggle.

Day 5: Proclaiming the Gospel with Excellence

Scripture: *Acts 1:1 – "In my former book, Theophilus, I wrote about all that Jesus began to do and to teach."*

Lesson: Luke's detailed writing in the Gospel of Luke and Acts ensured that future generations would know the truth of Christ. He documented history with precision and purpose.

Reflection: Are you communicating the Gospel clearly in your life—whether through words, actions, or testimony?

Challenge: Find a way to share Jesus today—whether by speaking, writing, or showing Christ's love through your actions.

Final Summary: What Luke Teaches Us

- **Day 1:** Use your gifts for God's kingdom—your profession and skills can glorify Him.

- **Day 2:** Seek truth—be diligent in studying God's Word.

- **Day 3:** Show compassion—care for those whom society overlooks.

- **Day 4:** Support others—stand by them even in their struggles.

- **Day 5:** Share the Gospel with excellence—ensure the message of Jesus is clearly seen in your life.

Life Application: Which lesson challenged you the most? How will you allow it to affect your decisions going forward? Pray for a heart like Luke's—dedicated to truth, compassion, and faithfulness in proclaiming the Gospel.

Chapter 76

Silas: Encouragement, Endurance, and Partnership in the Gospel

(Acts 15-18; I and II Thessalonians; I Peter 5)

Day 1: A Faithful Messenger of the Gospel

Scripture: *Acts 15:40 – "but Paul chose Silas and left, commended by the believers to the grace of the Lord."*

Lesson: Silas was chosen by Paul to accompany him on his missionary journeys. His willingness to serve showed his deep commitment to spreading the Gospel.

Reflection: Are you available and willing for God to use you in His work, no matter where He calls you?

Challenge: Pray today and ask God how He wants to use you in your church, workplace, community, or beyond. Be open to His leading.

Day 2: Singing in the Midnight Hour

Scripture: *Acts 16:25 – "About midnight Paul and Silas were praying and singing hymns to God, and the other prisoners were listening to them."*

Lesson: Even after being beaten and imprisoned, Silas worshiped God. His joy was not based on circumstances but on his faith in God's goodness.

Reflection: Do you praise God even in difficult times, or do you let trials steal your joy?

Challenge: No matter what you're facing today, choose to worship and thank God. Find a way to express gratitude in the middle of your circumstances.

Day 3: Enduring Hardship for the Gospel

Scripture: *1 Thessalonians 2:2 – "We had previously suffered and been treated outrageously in Philippi, as you know, but with the help of our God we dared to tell you His Gospel in the face of strong opposition."*

Lesson: Silas endured persecution but never backed down from proclaiming the Gospel. He knew that trials were part of following Christ.

Reflection: Are you willing to stand firm in your faith, even when you face opposition or discomfort?

Challenge: If you face resistance for your faith, respond with boldness and love. Stand firm in truth, knowing God strengthens you.

Day 4: Strengthening and Encouraging Others

Scripture: *Acts 15:32 – "Judas and Silas, who themselves were prophets, said much to encourage and strengthen the believers."*

Lesson: Silas wasn't just a missionary—he was an encourager. He used his words to build up others in their faith.

Reflection: Are you actively encouraging other believers, or do you focus more on your own struggles?

Challenge: Encourage someone today. Send a message, pray for them, or speak words of affirmation over their life.

Day 5: Serving in Partnership with Others

Scripture: *2 Corinthians 1:19 – "For the Son of God, Jesus Christ, who was preached among you by us—by me, Silas, and Timothy—was not 'Yes' and 'No,' but in Him it has always been 'Yes.'"*

Lesson: Silas worked alongside Paul and Timothy, showing that ministry is best done in partnership. He didn't seek personal glory but faithfully served with others.

Reflection: Are you working alongside others in God's mission, or are you trying to do everything alone?

Challenge: Find a way to partner with someone in ministry today. Support, encourage, or serve with a fellow believer in spreading the Gospel.

Final Summary: What Silas Teaches Us

- **Day 1:** Be available—say "yes" when God calls you.
- **Day 2:** Worship through trials—joy isn't based on circumstances.
- **Day 3:** Endure hardship—stand firm in the face of opposition.
- **Day 4:** Encourage others—build up fellow believers in faith.
- **Day 5:** Serve in partnership—ministry is stronger when done together.

Life Application: Which lesson stood out to you the most? How will you continue to carry it out? Pray for endurance, joy, and a heart that encourages others as you faithfully serve God.

Chapter 77

Timothy: Faithfulness, Discipleship, and Spiritual Strength

(Acts 16-20; Romans 16; I Corinthians 4,16; II Corinthians; Philippians; Colossians; I and II Thessalonians; I and II Timothy; Hebrews 13)

Day 1: A Strong Spiritual Foundation

Scripture: *2 Timothy 1:5 – "I am reminded of your sincere faith, which first lived in your grandmother Lois and in your mother Eunice and, I am persuaded, now lives in you also."*

Lesson: Timothy's faith was built on a strong foundation through the influence of his mother and grandmother. God often uses others to help shape our faith.

Reflection: Who has been a spiritual mentor in your life? Are you investing in the faith of others?

Challenge: Reach out to someone who has impacted your spiritual journey and thank them. If you're a mentor to someone, encourage them in their faith today. If you're not a mentor, ask the Lord to show you someone whom you could bring spiritual encouragement too.

Day 2: Overcoming Fear with Boldness

Scripture: *2 Timothy 1:7 – "For the Spirit God gave us does not make us timid, but gives us power, love, and self-discipline."*

Lesson: Timothy struggled with fear, but Paul reminded him that God had given him strength and courage. Fear should never stop us from living out our faith.

Reflection: Are you letting fear hold you back from sharing your faith or stepping into God's calling or purpose for you?

Challenge: Do something today that stretches your faith—whether sharing Jesus with someone, praying boldly, or stepping outside your comfort zone.

Day 3: Being an Example to Others

Scripture: *1 Timothy 4:12 – "Don't let anyone look down on you because you are young, but set an example for the believers in speech, in conduct, in love, in faith, and in purity."*

Lesson: Paul encouraged Timothy to be a role model, no matter his age. Spiritual maturity is shown through godly character, not just knowledge.

Reflection: Are you setting an example in your words, actions, love, and faith?

Challenge: Choose one area (speech, conduct, love, faith, or purity) to intentionally reflect Christ today.

Day 4: Staying Rooted in Scripture

Scripture: *2 Timothy 3:16-17 – "All Scripture is God-breathed and is useful for teaching, rebuking, correcting, and training in righteousness, so that the servant of God may be thoroughly equipped for every good work."*

Lesson: Paul reminded Timothy that God's Word is the foundation of a strong faith. Knowing Scripture equips us for every challenge.

Reflection: How much time do you spend in God's Word? Is it guiding your decisions and shaping your life?

Challenge: Commit to reading at least one chapter of Scripture today. Let it speak into your life and change how you live.

Day 5: Fighting the Good Fight of Faith

Scripture: *1 Timothy 6:12 – "Fight the good fight of the faith. Take hold of the eternal life to which you were called…"*

Lesson: Timothy was reminded that faith requires endurance. Following Christ is a battle against distractions, sin, and discouragement.

Reflection: Are you actively fighting for your faith, or have you become complacent?

Challenge: Strengthen your faith today—whether through prayer, resisting temptation, or encouraging someone else in their walk with Christ.

Final Summary: What Timothy Teaches Us

- **Day 1:** Build a strong foundation—learn from spiritual mentors and invest in others.
- **Day 2:** Overcome fear—God has given you boldness and strength.
- **Day 3:** Be an example—live in a way that reflects Christ.
- **Day 4:** Stay rooted in Scripture—it is your guide and strength.
- **Day 5:** Fight the good fight—faith requires perseverance and action.

Life Application: Which lesson resonated with you the most? How will you put it into practice going forward? Pray for boldness, wisdom, and endurance as you live out your faith and impact others.

Chapter 78

Apollos: Passion, Learning, and Boldly Proclaiming Christ

(Acts 18-19; I Corinthians 1,3-4,16; Titus 3)

Day 1: Passion for God's Word

Scripture: *Acts 18:24-25* – *"Meanwhile a Jew named Apollos, a native of Alexandria, came to Ephesus. He was a learned man, with a thorough knowledge of the Scriptures. He had been instructed in the way of the Lord, and he spoke with great fervor and taught about Jesus accurately, though he knew only the baptism of John."*

Lesson: Apollos was passionate about God's Word and taught it with enthusiasm. He didn't just have knowledge—he had zeal for spreading truth.

Reflection: Are you passionate about learning and sharing God's Word, or is your faith lukewarm?

Challenge: Dedicate time today to study Scripture deeply. Find one way to share what you learn with someone else.

Day 2: A Willingness to Learn and Grow

Scripture: *Acts 18:26* – *"He began to speak boldly in the synagogue. When Priscilla and Aquila heard him, they invited him to their home and explained to him the way of God more adequately."*

Lesson: Even though Apollos was knowledgeable, he was still humble enough to receive correction and deeper teaching. Growth requires a teachable spirit.

Reflection: Are you open to learning from others, even when you think you know a lot?

Challenge: Seek out wisdom today—whether from Scripture, a mentor, or a trusted believer. Be intentional about growing in your faith with humility.

Day 3: Boldly Proclaiming the Gospel

Scripture: *Acts 18:28 – "For he vigorously refuted his Jewish opponents in public debate, proving from the Scriptures that Jesus was the Messiah."*

Lesson: Apollos didn't shy away from speaking truth. He used Scripture to defend the Gospel and was fearless in proclaiming Christ.

Reflection: Are you confident in sharing your faith, or do you hesitate out of fear or uncertainty?

Challenge: Look for an opportunity today to share your faith or your testimony of what God has done in your life—whether in conversation, online, or through an act of love.

Day 4: Building Up the Church, Not Seeking Fame

Scripture: *1 Corinthians 3:6 – "I planted the seed, Apollos watered it, but God has been making it grow."*

Lesson: Paul made it clear that Apollos' role in the church was important, but ultimately, God brings the growth. Apollos served faithfully without seeking personal glory.

Reflection: Are you seeking recognition for your service, or are you content to let God receive the glory?

Challenge: Serve someone today in a way that brings glory to God rather than yourself.

Day 5: Strengthening the Faith of Others

Scripture: *Acts 18:27 – "When Apollos wanted to go to Achaia, the brothers and sisters encouraged him and wrote to the disciples there to welcome him. When he arrived, he was a great help to those who by grace had believed."*

Lesson: Apollos not only shared the Gospel—he strengthened the faith of other believers. He used his gifts to build up the church.

Reflection: Are you helping others grow in their faith, or do you focus only on your own spiritual journey?

Challenge: Encourage and strengthen a fellow believer today. Pray for them, share a word of encouragement, or support them in their faith journey.

Final Summary: What Apollos Teaches Us

- **Day 1:** Be passionate about God's Word—study and share it.

- **Day 2:** Stay teachable—growth requires humility.

- **Day 3:** Boldly proclaim the Gospel—don't shy away from speaking truth.

- **Day 4:** Serve for God's glory, not personal recognition.

- **Day 5:** Strengthen others in their faith—help build up the church.

Life Application: Which lesson do you need to practice the most? How will you incorporate it moving forward? Pray for boldness, humility, and a heart that strengthens others in the faith like Apollos.

THE BIG PICTURE

GODLY AND UNGODLY CHARACTER TRAITS OF MEN THROUGHOUT SCRIPTURE

Top 10 Positive Character Traits to Follow:

1. **Unwavering Faith in God**

   - Trusting in God despite challenges, uncertainties, or opposition.

   - **Examples:**

     - **Caleb** – Believed in God's promise and was willing to fight for the Promised Land.

     - **Hezekiah** – Trusted God to deliver Judah from the Assyrians.

     - **Daniel** – Continued to pray despite the threat of the lions' den.

2. **Obedience to God's Commands**

   - Following God's instructions without hesitation or compromise.

   - **Examples:**

     - **Noah** – Built the ark as God commanded, even when it seemed impossible.

     - **Josiah** – Restored true worship and removed idols from Israel.

     - **Philip the Evangelist** – Obeyed the Spirit and went to preach to the Ethiopian eunuch.

3. **Courage to Stand for Truth**

    ◦ Standing for God's truth despite fear, persecution, or opposition.

    ◦ **Examples:**

        • **Gideon** – Trusted God and led 300 men against a massive enemy army.

        • **Shadrach, Meshach, and Abednego** – Refused to bow to the golden idol.

        • **Stephen** – Boldly preached Christ even when facing martyrdom.

4. **Humility and Dependence on God**

    ◦ Acknowledging that all success and strength come from God, not oneself.

    ◦ **Examples:**

        • **Moses** – Led Israel with humility, seeking God's guidance.

        • **Hezekiah** – Turned to God in prayer when his kingdom was threatened.

        • **John the Baptist** – Said, "He must become greater; I must become less."

5. **Prayer as a Foundation for Life**

    ◦ Seeking God daily in prayer and relying on Him for wisdom and strength.

    ◦ **Examples:**

        • **Elijah** – Prayed fervently, and God responded powerfully.

        • **Daniel** – Prayed three times daily, even when it was outlawed.

        • **Nehemiah** – Prayed before every major decision.

6. **Perseverance and Endurance in Trials**

    ◦ Remaining faithful despite hardship, opposition, or long waits.

    ◦ **Examples:**

        • **Job** – Remained faithful to God despite losing everything.

- **Joseph** – Endured betrayal and imprisonment before being elevated by God.

- **Paul** – Continued preaching despite beatings, imprisonment, and hardship.

7. **Studying and Teaching God's Word**

    - Dedicating oneself to learning, living, and teaching the Scriptures.

    - **Examples:**

        - **Jehoshaphat** – Sent teachers throughout Judah to spread God's Word.

        - **Ezra** – Devoted himself to studying and teaching the Law.

        - **Timothy** – Continued in faithfulness to the Scriptures, encouraged by Paul.

8. **Generosity and Kindness to Others**

    - Using resources, time, and influence to bless and care for others.

    - **Examples:**

        - **Boaz** – Showed kindness to Ruth and provided for her.

        - **Barnabas** – Sold land to support the early church.

        - **Cornelius** – Gave generously to the poor and sought God.

9. **Wisdom and Godly Leadership**

    - Leading with integrity, seeking counsel, and making decisions based on God's will.

    - **Examples:**

        - **Jethro** – Gave Moses wise counsel to delegate leadership responsibilities.

        - **Solomon** – Asked for wisdom to rule his people justly.

        - **Nehemiah** – Led the rebuilding of Jerusalem with prayer and strategy.

10. **Repentance and Seeking Forgiveness**

    - Acknowledging sin, turning back to God, and striving to live righteously.

    - **Examples:**

        - **David** – Repented sincerely after sinning with Bathsheba.

        - **Zacchaeus** - Restored money he had wrongly taken as a tax collector.

        - **Peter** – Wept and returned to Jesus after denying Him.

Top 5 Negative Character Traits to Avoid:

1. **Pride and Self-Reliance**

    - Trusting in one's own strength instead of depending on God.

    - **Examples:**

        - **Jacob** – Deceived his father to steal his brother's birthright.

        - **King Saul** – Acted in pride, making rash decisions without God's approval.

        - **Hezekiah (later in life)** – Showed off his treasures to Babylon instead of giving glory to God.

2. **Compromise and Idolatry**

    - Allowing worldly desires or ungodly influences to take precedence over devotion to God.

    - **Examples:**

        - **Adam** – Chose to eat from the one tree God told him not to eat from.

        - **Solomon (later in life)** – Allowed his foreign wives to turn his heart from God.

        - **King Ahab** – Married Jezebel and introduced widespread idol worship.

3. **Fear of People Over Fear of God**

    ◦ Making decisions based on pleasing others instead of obeying God.

    ◦ **Examples:**

        - **Aaron** – Created the golden calf to appease the Israelites.

        - **King Saul** – Making a sacrifice that only Samuel should have made to please the people.

        - **Pontius Pilate** – Knew Jesus was innocent but sentenced Him to please the crowd.

4. **Greed and Selfish Ambition**

    ◦ Pursuing wealth, status, or personal gain at the expense of righteousness.

    ◦ **Examples:**

        - **Balaam** – Desired riches and tried to manipulate God's will.

        - **Gehazi (Elisha's servant)** – Took riches deceitfully and was punished with leprosy.

        - **Judas Iscariot** – Betrayed Jesus for thirty pieces of silver.

5. **Ignoring God's Warnings and Refusing to Repent**

    ◦ Persisting in sin despite receiving multiple opportunities to turn back.

    ◦ **Examples:**

        - **Balaam** – God warned him multiple times, even through a donkey, but he persisted to go against God's plan.

        - **King Saul** – Never repented from any of the warnings and rebukes from the prophet Samuel.

        - **King Ahab** – Ignored warning after warning from multiple prophets until he brought destruction on himself and his entire family.

Final Reflection and Application

The lives of these biblical figures teach us profound lessons about faith, obedience, and character. As you reflect on these traits:

Ask Yourself:

- Which positive traits do I need to develop more in my life?
- Which negative traits have I been struggling with, and how can I overcome them?
- What practical steps can I take to align more with God's will?

Prayer: *Lord, shape my heart to reflect Your character. Help me to be strong in faith, steadfast in obedience, and humble in spirit. Protect me from pride, compromise, and fear of man. Let my life be a testimony of Your grace and truth. In Jesus' name, Amen.*

Printed in Dunstable, United Kingdom